PRAISE FOR
THE AI ECOSYSTEMS REVOLUTION

In *The AI Ecosystems Revolution,* Joe masterfully addresses the complexities of modern global supply chains and the transformative power of AI-driven collaboration. This book is an essential read for business leaders navigating the intersection of technology and supply chain management. Joe's insights on real-time collaboration will undoubtedly reshape how companies approach operational efficiency and innovation, making it a must-read for forward-thinking executives.

—Domenico Passannanti
Partner, Ernst & Young

The COVID pandemic exposed all the risks and limitations of a globally interconnected supply chain. The two most frequently asked questions by consumers and businesspeople were "Where's my stuff?" followed by "When am I going to get my stuff?" If you asked the supermarket owner, the consumer goods manufacturer, or the logistics carrier, they were unable to provide you with an answer beyond "We don't know." In *The AI Ecosystems Revolution,* Joe Hudicka lays out a plan to leverage collaboration and new artificial intelligence technologies to help companies improve their planning and logistics processes, and speed up their response times.

—Bruce Richardson
Chief Enterprise Strategist, Salesforce

The AI Ecosystems Revolution is a timely and transformative guide for anyone looking to stay ahead in the rapidly evolving world of supply chain management. Joe Hudicka masterfully illustrates how AI and real-time data ecosystems can reshape the way organizations operate, turning traditional supply chains into dynamic, predictive systems that foster agility and efficiency. The practical strategies, backed by real-world case studies, offer a roadmap to navigate the complexities of modern logistics while embracing innovation. This book is a must-read for leaders who aim to leverage technology to drive operational excellence and future-proof their businesses.

—Erez Agmoni
Global Head of Innovation, MAERSK

Joe's disruptive thinking around connected conversations™ marks a vital shift from product-driven to people-centric technological solutions. His book emphasizes the importance of digitizing communications but, more importantly, how replacing clicks with conversations serves a fundamental human need, driving fast adoption and transforming the way we connect and drive societal progress in the world of global supply—right now.

—Wolfgang Lehmacher

Board Member, Executive Advisor, and Business Angel, Wolfgang Lehmacher; Founder and Cohost, Supply Chain Innovation Network, Maritime Informatics Institute; Former Director and Head of Supply Chain and Transport Industries, World Economic Forum

The rapid development in AI has generated dozens of books about it—from fundamental definitions through advanced concepts on its projected impacts on business and societies. Joe has produced a book using the global logistics of goods to stimulate thinking and inspirations on major complexity in supply chain management. Even as Nearshoring and other global shifts in production and distribution occur, goods will always need to flow from source (origin) to customers (destination). Joe's conversational writing style is appealing and easy to read and understand by all readers. I highly recommend this book to anyone interested in AI, in Logistics and Supply Chain innovation, or what lies ahead.

—Gene Tyndall

Co-Founder, eMATE Consulting; Former President, Ryder Global Supply Chain Solutions; co-author, Breakthrough Supply Chains *(McGraw-Hill, 2023)*

If you're diving into the world of AI and its impact on the global supply chain, *The AI Ecosystems Revolution* by Joe Hudicka is an essential read. Hudicka presents complex concepts with clarity, making them accessible—whether you're a beginner or an expert in the fields of computer science, AI, logistics, and the global supply chains. The book has many real-world examples of companies and organizations and how they've addressed change management in the past, and how AI will be one of the most dramatic changes they'll ever confront. It's an invaluable resource for anyone looking to deepen their understanding and expertise with the power of AI and real-time data to streamline processes, mitigate risks, and drive operational excellence.

—Matthew Grover
Former EVP & Chief Revenue Officer, Altice USA

THE AI ECOSYSTEMS REVOLUTION

THE AI ECOSYSTEMS REVOLUTION

TRANSFORMING

THE GLOBAL SUPPLY CHAIN

THROUGH REAL-TIME

COLLABORATION

JOE HUDICKA

Forbes | Books

Copyright © 2025 by Joseph R. Hudicka, MBA.

Published by Forbes Books, Charleston, South Carolina.
An imprint of Advantage Media Group.

Forbes Books is a registered trademark, and the Forbes Books colophon is a trademark of Forbes Media, LLC.

Printed in the United States of America.

10 9 8 7 6 5 4 3 2 1

ISBN: 979-8-88750-566-4 (Hardcover)
ISBN: 979-8-88750-567-1 (eBook)

Library of Congress Control Number: 2024924102

Cover design by Matthew Morse.
Layout design by Ruthie Wood.

This custom publication is intended to provide accurate information and the opinions of the author in regard to the subject matter covered. It is sold with the understanding that the publisher, Forbes Books, is not engaged in rendering legal, financial, or professional services of any kind. If legal advice or other expert assistance is required, the reader is advised to seek the services of a competent professional.

Since 1917, Forbes has remained steadfast in its mission to serve as the defining voice of entrepreneurial capitalism. Forbes Books, launched in 2016 through a partnership with Advantage Media, furthers that aim by helping business and thought leaders bring their stories, passion, and knowledge to the forefront in custom books. Opinions expressed by Forbes Books authors are their own. To be considered for publication, please visit **books.Forbes.com**.

For my superhero and his sidekick,

Without whom I wouldn't be…

For my wonder twin,

Who optimizes all I wish to be…

For my rock band,

Who scores this amazing journey…

And my superfans

Creating this bigger future I see.

You know who you are.

CONTENTS

ACKNOWLEDGMENTS

I would like to extend my heartfelt gratitude to the music industry, whose vibrant tapestry of sounds, rhythms, and stories has profoundly shaped my creative journey. From the legendary artists who have inspired me with their genius to the countless songwriters and producers whose passion fuels our shared love for music, thank you for your unwavering dedication to the craft.

Music has not only been a source of motivation but also a guiding light in times of uncertainty. It has provided the backdrop to my most cherished memories and has fueled my imagination in ways I could never have anticipated. Each note, each lyric, and each beat has woven itself into the fabric of my life, encouraging me to push boundaries and explore new horizons.

To the labels, the promoters, and the unsung heroes behind the scenes, your hard work and vision have created a world where creativity can thrive. I am endlessly grateful for the impact you have made, not only in my life but in the lives of countless others.

As you read through these pages, I invite you to immerse yourself in the accompanying playlist that has been a constant companion throughout my writing process. Each song echoes the themes and emotions woven into this book, enhancing the experience and inviting you to feel the rhythm of my journey.

Thank you for reminding us all of the power of art to uplift, connect, and transform.

Enjoy listening to **THE AI ECOSYSTEMS™ REVOLUTION MUSIC COMPANION PLAYLIST**.

Follow the QR code to your preferred streaming platform:

INTRODUCTION

It's the end of the world as we know it, and I feel fine.

—"IT'S THE END OF THE WORLD AS WE KNOW IT (AND I FEEL FINE)," R.E.M.

OK, look. I know you came here to talk about the future of the supply chain. I get it. But bear with me for a sec, because this all will make a lot more sense once you get some background.

I grew up as one of those 1980s kids who had no clue about the excesses of the era. You remember that time, right? When Wall Street was booming (until it wasn't) and everyone was told they should buy bigger houses and bigger cars and party all the time. There's a reason why the 1980s are obsessed over and were eventually showcased in the 2000s in nostalgic TV specials. However, I came from a factory family. My parents worked very hard, five days a week (oftentimes more), just to make ends meet.

Kids can pick up on the signals that life is transmitting around them. Sure, I wanted all the great toys I saw in TV commercials, but when I paged through the Sears catalog around Thanksgiving to compile my annual wish list for Santa, there was no chance that any of those things would end up under the tree. Really, holding that catalog was as close as I was going to get to owning any of those things that I wanted so badly.

But then, sometime in the 1980s, I had that one magical Christmas—the one we all fantasize about.

As was typical for our family, we would wake up on Christmas morning, and the gift opening would naturally begin with me, the youngest. I tore through each and every gift, riding that gleeful chemical high that moments like this deliver to your brain, and then, just as suddenly, it was over. I thanked my parents, like I always did, but it rang a bit more hollow than in prior years. It just wasn't the same. There was this ache building deep within me, and it was growing with every second.

Then my dad, a man with a huge heart but very few words, encouraged me to open my stocking. This was a formality that I had to attend to, but everybody knows that the stockings don't hold the good stuff. I did my best to steer away from the negative thoughts and feelings welling up inside of me while, one by one, I pulled each and every piece of candy out of the stocking.

But then, as I reached the bottom, I found a little handwritten note from my dad. He wasn't a greeting card guy, so this little piece of paper was the best I was going to get. I carefully unfolded the note, and inside was a message from my father. I can't remember the specifics, but the essence was about reminding me just how hard life is and how we must work hard just to survive. That also means we must appreciate everything and every little moment.

My father's words burned this memory into my heart and head forever. He praised me for simply being my true self and explained how proud he was of who I was at that moment and who I was becoming.

I'm an overly sentimental person, and at that particular moment, I was very much experiencing a ton of feelings. In the last sentence of the note, my dad's letter took a turn toward the future. He shared with me that sometimes, if we work hard enough, dreams can come true, and one of those dreams just might be hiding upstairs under my very own bed.

I raced to the back of the house, taking two steps at a time up to the top story, almost doing a baseball slide to my bed. And there it was, the gift of gifts and one I had hoped and dreamed of all year: a ColecoVision.

Up until that moment, I had only touched one arcade game in my life. I'd only seen one home gaming system—and now I had one of my very own. Have you ever seen that video of the Nintendo 64 kids? If you haven't seen "Nintendo Sixty-FOOOOOOOOOOOUR," the one-minute-six-second clip on YouTube with over twenty-five million views,[1] understand that it's two kids, and one in particular, who is *very* excited to get the latest console. I would've put them to shame.

I invested every moment I could find that year trying to master all the games in my burgeoning collection. I'd scour every store seeking my next game challenge—and I absolutely loved every bit of it. This wasn't like the TV shows, books, or movies that made up the previous part of my youth. This was entertainment I could interact with, and that was amazing.

My gratitude toward my father was already huge, but this Christmas he elevated himself in my eyes to a godlike status. Little

---

1   raw64life, "Nintendo Sixty-FOOOOOOOOOOOUR," March 26, 2006, YouTube video, 1:06, https://youtu.be/pFlcqWQVVuU.

did I know that he would double down the following year, getting me a Commodore 64—my first personal computer.

Now to be fully transparent, I think of myself as an extremely lazy person. While I never shy away from work or the hard stuff, if I can find a path of least resistance, I'm there.

So while, at first, I treated the Commodore 64 as an alternative gaming platform to the ColecoVision, it turned out that my dad had ulterior motives.

Back then there were a lot of magazines dedicated to personal computing. You could even get complete programs within their pages, whether they were written down for you to copy over or included on a floppy disk. My dad took me to the store and had me look at those issues, all containing tons of information that I knew nothing about. As I flipped through them, I began to see those programs and scripts, and I started wondering what they were all about.

See, the base model Commodore, as well as other personal computers, did not yet come with permanent storage. You had to buy those devices separately. And since my father knew even less than I did about this stuff, I didn't have any way to hold on to the work or scripts that I entered.

But what I could do was turn the computer on, rekey the program from the magazine into the computer's memory, run it, and see the results appear on the screen. It was a whole new level of magic for me. I could feed ideas into this thing, and it could act on them.

That was what I did for a long time. I wasn't working on creating my own scripts but rather feeding other people's ideas into the computer from the magazines. But eventually, Dad's true intentions became clear. One night, over dinner, he said, "Hey, bud, do you think you can make the computer pick the winning lottery numbers for me?"

I laughed, immediately thinking about how the act of guessing winning numbers via a computer is no different from a human guessing the numbers themselves. But as it turns out, he was serious.

So I pulled out the programming guide for the BASIC language, which came with the Commodore 64. It took me quite some time, as I had to learn how to define my own variables for things, such as how many numbers are in the lottery and how many get selected. Then I needed to learn how to select a random number out of that set and how to create a loop that could repeat the random selection process until a full set of numbers was chosen. There were other steps I had to learn as well, but you get my drift.

Dad was hoping for alchemy, and in a way, that was exactly what he got. Because from that moment on, I looked at these personal computing and entertainment devices very differently. They weren't just a way to play games and mess around but also a pole I could lever into position so that I could make the world go 'round.

I realized these personal electronic devices weren't just about creating value for myself. Now they would also create value for others, such as trying to help my dad win the lottery. Even though I was just a little kid and I didn't really put all of those pieces together, I knew these technologies could give me the ability to discover and deliver even more ways to create value. And that, in turn, would return value to me as well. But putting all that into action would take even more time.

I became jaded with education at the end of the first marking period of second grade. I've always had this innate competitive drive; I wanted to be the first and the fastest in everything. And for some reason, over the summer between first and second grade, I decided I was going to get straight As on my report card. What kind of eight-year-old chooses that?

I went into the school year confident, and by the end I thought everything was going according to plan. But when the report card came in, hidden among all of those As was one D—for writing—specifically, penmanship.

This enraged me. I stormed the half-mile walk home. I didn't talk to my family, and I couldn't eat. I needed to confront my teacher.

I waited at Mrs. Simington's desk for a full thirty minutes before she arrived and greeted me with a smile, which I could not match in that moment.

I looked at her and said, "Mrs. Simington, I just have one question for you about my report card. How do you know I learned enough to earn As in all of these classes when you couldn't read a single thing I wrote?" I repeatedly banged my left index finger on her desk, drawing her focus to the Writing Grade.

A quick aside: Did you know that back then left-handed kids were given pencils that were like triple the thickness of normal pencils? As though it weren't bad enough that us left-handers have to drag our writing hands across everything we write, smearing it as we go.

But there it was. My teacher couldn't read my handwriting, and that wasn't entirely my fault either. It all seemed so arbitrary. There was no black or white, only gray. This was a clarifying moment for me. I realized there had to be a better way for me to learn and write. I had no clue what those ways would be, but I had to focus to make them my new reality and as soon as possible. Now I would live in the gray.

From ages eight through eighteen, I gamified schooling in every way I possibly could. I studied what I believed the teachers wanted to grade me on rather than what they were trying to teach me. I learned how to learn what I chose to learn while also meeting whatever learning expectations that the outside world placed on me.

And then in seventh grade, I was eligible to take my first programming class. In true Joe form, I spent most classes on the Apple IIc or IIe, playing *Super Bowl Sunday*. I collaborated with friends who were actually interested in completing deliverables and figured out pretty quickly that no teacher was thinking about how to identify a "digital signature" of programming to determine whether two students each wrote their own programs or one wrote it and made two copies.

As I got into high school, math took a really bad turn for me, as letters and symbols started getting mashed up with my numbers. I plummeted from ninety-third percentile in the country to ... Well, I don't want to talk about it.

I finally hit rock bottom on day one in geometry, when my new teacher sadly chose to single me out to explain how I could measure the tree she drew on the chalkboard using a stick figure version of me off to the left of the plant.

It turns out she wanted me to magically enter this enlightened mathematical state where I'd see the invisible triangle formed by the height of the tree, the ground distance between the tree and my stick figure representation, and the distance between me and the height of the tree. Unfortunately, this particular math teacher came from the all-too-common school of "I'm smarter than you—figure it out or fail," and fail I did.

But not before giving her my answer.

Just before I walked out of her class, I explained for everyone to hear, "Based on what little you've taught me about measuring the height of this tree and my own personal knowledge I'm bringing into your class, I suppose I'd have to cut the tree down and drag a measuring device from one end of the tree to the other. But my question to you is, How tall could that tree have become if only you had taught me a better way?"

As you can see, these early years of education, at least in the way it was available when I was a kid, did not work for me. I rejected it pretty soundly.

This early observation is what guided me to choose a college where I could apply personal computing technology to solve business problems. Computer science was not for me; I was, and still am to an extent, terrified of the inner workings of a computer. (I literally told the dean of Rider College that I chose his school because when it came to computing, I simply wanted to turn the computer on, see pretty lights flash, and use it to build business solutions that I can sell.)

Back then there was a single method of teaching: read the book, take the test, write the paper, and then pass or fail. I was *not* a reader, which was a problem.

But what I could do was begin charting my own educational course load. I could, for example, match my software development interests with market needs. It was a transactional relationship to me, with this just being one of the methods of payment.

Now while it wouldn't put food on my table, the other payment came in the form of experience, and I got a lot of that. I was building business solutions that delivered new value while simultaneously building my résumé.

My first job out of college was as a consultant for a company that made the machines that make Intel microprocessors. I designed a bill of materials solution for these very complex machines, which are made of many subassemblies. No software could do that at the time.

To put it in more common terms, think about building bicycles. How many frames do you need? How many wheels? Are the wheels the same or different? What about reflectors, seats, and everything else? The bill of materials is like a recipe for manufacturing, and that's what I did for these machines.

I then pivoted into work that became part of the US Department of Defense with the United States Coast Guard, solving for the global supply and maintenance chain of coast guard transport assets, such as choppers and cutters. For that, I needed to know when a piece of equipment needed maintenance, get it scheduled to be in a location where it can get that maintenance, have the right parts and materials available in that moment, and find certified technicians to complete the job. It was tough work, but it taught me a lot.

Next came the dot-com era, just after I wrote a book with Osborne McGraw-Hill/Oracle press.[2] (It's called *Oracle8 Design Using UML Object Modeling*, and while I understand it's not the catchiest title, it served a purpose. This was Oracle's big architectural shift from relational to object relational, which is far more flexible—though that flexibility is a double-edged sword, because it takes a very savvy architect to leverage these greater capabilities in a meaningful way.) Instead of needing to get consumer products to thousands of retail stores worldwide, now millions of consumers had their very own virtual stores via their computers, right in their homes. How does this change the landscape of taking orders? How does this change the number and design of the distribution centers that now have to become fulfillment centers? Who's gonna deliver all these packages directly to homes?

The common thread here became the supply chain, and through my unique experience set, I found myself ahead of the market. And I felt great because, as it turns out, I only knew (and know) how to live in the future.

One of my favorite books on this subject is *Change by Design: How Design Thinking Transforms Organizations and Inspires Innovation*

---

2   Paul Dorsey and Joseph R. Hudicka, *Oracle8 Design Using UML Object Modeling* (Osborne/McGraw-Hill, 1999).

by Tim Brown. While this is a big topic (enough for a book, naturally), the gist is that design should be human centered, so you understand the needs of users and create solutions based on that. Ken Anderson expands on that concept in his research, noting that design should be human centric by taking into account the experiences of all humans affected by the outcome, each of whom may be impacted differently.

A key talking point is how our societal systems need to change from how they were created. Education, transportation, industrial complexes—all these and more should move away from design for the sake of design and instead solve the problems we have as people. They need to address the issues present today, including health, poverty, and education. How could we take the ideas and knowledge we have today and apply them to society at large?[3]

I want to expand things even further and use this design thinking exercise to make those kinds of changes worldwide. First, I want to adopt a "less is more" principle in everything we pursue from here on out. Second, let's not just think about those results but actually activate them. As a future-thinking person, I believe it's go big or go home—24-7. And that's also why I've chosen to take on one of the largest challenges in our world today, specifically in the field of global supply chain management.

It's time to break the chains that bind this process. For decades, retailers, shippers, manufacturers, suppliers, and transporters have played this game of poker, hiding vital information about their future demands from the very partners their success depends on. We need to get out of that rut and shift from human-centered business processes (like a software program for a salesperson to record notes from meeting they've had with prospective customers) to human-centric ecosystems

---

3   Tim Brown and Barry Katz, *Change by Design: How Design Thinking Transforms Organizations and Inspires Innovation* (Harper Business, 2019).

(think about software that transcribes meeting notes, summarizes key highlights, and automatically shares those notes with the right people in your team). Plus, we're going to talk about the amazing advances in AI that've been made over the past few years and see how they integrate into the logistics systems that we already have—or how they can replace them.

Together, we're going to take a journey and, along the way, maybe take a few concepts from Charles Dickens's *A Christmas Carol* and visit the ghosts of the past and look to the ghosts of the future. Eventually, we'll get to our future together, and we hope that we meet in your present. It's my gift to you and the reason I've broken the book down into the following three sections:

1. Diagnose

2. Predict

3. Prescribe

There are also three core disciplines that we'll pick up along the way: innovation, creativity, and entrepreneurship. You'll see how I learned to weave them together to help discover big ideas, build momentum beneath them, and launch them into value creation. Then you can use these same tools to do the same thing for yourself.

I'm also not the only voice present in this book. That's because I've spent some time talking to people I consider to be my mentors, my friends in the industry, and folks who I generally admire.

When it comes time for you to meet them, you'll know. I'll do my flowery introduction and really puff them up a bunch, then we'll roll into their insights. My hope is that you enjoy their thoughts as much as I have, because I feel like they make a big impact on the book itself.

Of course, you may wonder what any of this has to do with an R.E.M. song from the 1990s, so let me explain.

Music is a huge part of my life and has been since I was a kid. I listen to it every day, and I love tearing apart the lyrics to try to understand the message of the artist. I'm not alone in this regard; there are other weirdos like me who love music this much. Maybe you're one of them.

In the process of writing this book, I thought about how some of those lyrics, while not intentionally written this way, do apply to the shipping and logistics industry. So to give credit to those artists and their contributions to my life and these concepts, they're included at the beginning of every chapter. It's a way that I can combine one of my passions with another, and hopefully, it brings you a little bit of joy too.

This book isn't just about the future. It's also about where we came from, where we are, and where we're going. Get ready, because it's going to be a fun ride.

CHAPTER ONE

You Are Here

It's been a long, a long time coming ...

—"A CHANGE IS GONNA COME," SAM COOKE

Let's take a trip back in time to the 1990s. Remember then? Back when you had a binder full of CDs that you'd keep under your car's passenger seat so thieves wouldn't find them, but inevitably, they would anyway? Yeah, those were good times. And those CDs made the music industry a lot of money. So much so that they felt unstoppable.

Enter Napster in 1999. Napster was a peer-to-peer file-sharing service that allowed users to share and download music for free. All of a sudden, everyone with an internet connection could get any album ever produced anywhere, and it didn't cost them a dime. On the other side of the coin, the music industry didn't make any money off the downloads either. But artists faced an even bigger problem. It's tough enough to make it in the music industry as it is, but when you take away one of their most significant earning points, it gets even harder.

From the industry's perspective, this came out of nowhere. The world's concept of how music was consumed shifted dramatically, which—arguably more importantly—also affected its value, and sales dropped with it.

One of the most vocal opponents of Napster and illegal downloading became Lars Ulrich, the drummer for the band Metallica. This became such an issue that they took it to court, filing in the US District Court for the Northern District of California on April 13, 2000.[4] They alleged Racketeer Influenced and Corrupt Organizations (commonly known as RICO) and copyright infringement. This wouldn't be the only case against Napster, either, as soon, more music companies and artists would sue.

Eventually, this was all too much for Napster, which shut down in 2001. They would later revive the brand name, and you can still find it today on the web, but the company is now a streaming service similar to Spotify and Apple Music. Now the functional end of Napster as a peer-to-peer service didn't solve the industry's challenges. Instead, it signaled the rise of digital music consumption. Suddenly, the traditional business model for the industry that had reigned for decades was no longer viable.

This change, even though they were forced into it, meant they had to acknowledge that the digital age offered new opportunities for reaching audiences and generating revenue. One of the bigger realizations they had was the reimagining of live concerts. Previously, they

---

4   "Metallica v. Napster, Inc.," Wikipedia, September 13, 2023, https://en.wikipedia.org/wiki/Metallica_v._Napster,_Inc.

were just a way to promote album sales. But now they could evolve into what it is today, the industry's most lucrative revenue stream.[5]

Because live experiences are so rare compared with the ubiquity of digital music, this allowed artists and record labels to capitalize on their unique value. They could do these huge and elaborate productions built to give fans unforgettable experiences—often accompanied by high ticket prices, exclusive merch, and VIP packages.

This gave the music industry a way to offset the losses from those declining physical sales and also pumped up the importance of live performances as a distinct and valuable aspect of an artist's career. This whole process shows how resilient an industry can be when forced to come up with creative solutions to a problem.

Today, digital platforms aren't the adversary of the music industry but a vital partner. The value of music is celebrated both in its digital and live forms. This creates a dynamic ecosystem that is a bit more flexible than the previous model.

Digital Disruption

Of course, the music industry wasn't the only one affected by the digital revolution. This is particularly the case in the realm of transportation logistics, which has a hierarchy called party logistics that contains five levels, known as first-party logistics (1PL) through fifth-party logistics (5PL). Let me lay out this complex system with a fairly simplified take.

5PL logistics is typically considered to be the manufacturers or suppliers to manufacturers. This is the foundation level, so it's basically

---

5   Ethan Millman, "Taylor Swift's Eras Tour Is the Highest-Grossing of All Time and First-Ever to Hit $1 Billion," *Rolling Stone,* December 8, 2023, https://www.rollingstone.com/music/music-news/taylor-swift-eras-tour-highest-grossing-all-time-1-billion-1234921647/.

who's making stuff. With second-party logistics (2PL), this is where suppliers come into the picture. 3PL refers to third-party logistics, which provide other services around and oftentimes including transportation. They do warehousing and distribution services and may even add other brand-focused value adds.

Then you have fourth-party logistics (4PL), which offer more value-based capabilities. They're usually not asset based like 1PL to 3PL, because they do not own the physical assets. They don't necessarily own the physical warehouses, but they get much more involved in their clients' direct business activities. Finally, there's 5PL. These take 4PL up a notch and become deeply involved to the point where they can negotiate with other service providers, such as the transporters, truck carriers, airlines, etc. They can plan and organize the overall logistical solutions on behalf of other parties. They have the ability to fortify and aggregate demand across all sorts of sources, as well as balance these supply relationships.

Basically, what you've got is a really interesting and super messy model that evolved over a seventy-year period. There have been big shifts over the years, such as the invention of containerized shipping by Malcolm McLean in 1956.[6]

But at this point, you're probably wondering how any of what I just told you connects to the music industry. Really, how does this matter to the world of global supply?

Bear with me for a sec with this analogy: Think about the various layers of logistics—1PL through 5PL—as a vertical layer cake. 5PL is the bottom layer on the table, the next one on top is 4PL, and so on. As each layer stacks up, it adds mass to the overall cake. The layers on

---

6   "Malcom McLean," Wikipedia, last edited August 14, 2024, https://en.wikipedia.org/ wiki/Malcom_McLean#:~:text=Malcolm%20Purcell%20McLean%20(November%20 14,half%20of%20the%20twentieth%20century.

the bottom, therefore, have more pressure on them than the ones at the top. 1PL feels no concerns, while 5PL seemingly has the weight of the world thrust upon them.

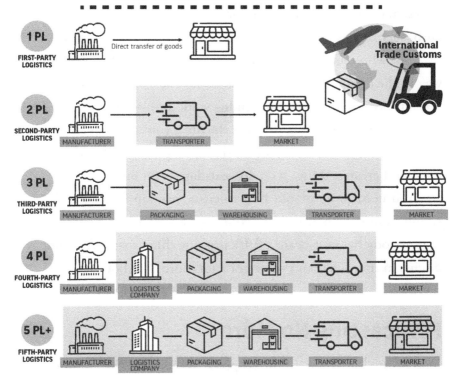

(As an aside, if you look hard enough, you'll find companies that present themselves as 7PLs. Really, anything 5PL and above is managed services and fully outsourced, full stop.)

Now think about how someone in 3PL would feel with all that pressure, which, in this case, is coming from digitalization. After all, 3PL companies don't necessarily own the assets. They don't necessarily own the strategic insights of supply and demand. They could get crushed pretty quickly if they didn't adapt. One way to do that is for 3PL organizations, and ones in similar spaces, to develop their own assets.

If they don't, they get crushed, just the same way we saw in the music industry. Sure, we can identify the names of the record companies that are still around and show how they reinvented themselves, and we can do the same for the ones that were kicked to the curb, such as Tower Records. Those are the big cats in the space.

But who remembers a smaller record company that also lost its way to the digital revolution? What about the artists who fell by the wayside because their contracts didn't work in this new world or who refused to go to streaming? Most of the time, you can't remember who they were, because these niche markets just got pushed aside for the latest and greatest thing. It's a dog-eat-dog world out there.

You need to figure out how to cross that gap for you and your supply company. Is it owning your own assets? Is it a new product that nobody has ever heard of? It's just one thing that we're going to discuss in this book, and we've got a lot more ahead of us.

Forecasting No More

One of the big tenets of the shipping industry is forecasting. The idea is that we have so much data on hand that we can predict what products are needed when and where; therefore we only have to prepare for that—and nothing else. You could compare this to a fisherman literally casting a single line into a vast sea and hoping to catch their limit. And while that worked for a long time, those days are numbered. The future of global supply demands resiliency, and hope is no longer acceptable.

Let's look at something that's kind of crazy that's going on in Saudi Arabia. Are you familiar with The Line? It's a part of a larger concept called NEOM, and it's nuts.

The Line is planned to be a 106-mile-long city[7] in the middle of the desert, in the Tabuk Province of Saudi Arabia.[8] As the name suggests, the concept imagines a metropolis that has a fixed width of 600 feet with a length of 106 miles, which would look like a straight line. Inside is everything you want a city to be. NEOM calls it "Zero Gravity Urbanism," and that means high-speed rail, no cars, and 100 percent renewable energy. Everything is stacked vertically, as opposed to being spread out like you see in most urban environments.

This is a controversial topic for so many reasons that I just don't care to get into, because frankly, that's not the point here. But the first thing I thought of when I heard about this concept was, "How are the people in The Line going to get their goods?" And as it turns out, they're revolutionizing that process too.

NEOM has a region they're calling Oxagon, which is just nuts, and the best way to think about it is like *SimCity*. Do you remember that game? It's still around (and it's a lot of fun), but to give you an idea of how it works, you have to build up this city by zoning areas as either residential, commercial, or industrial. The interaction between these spaces makes things more complicated, and it's all based on the real world.

For example, say you put a power plant right next to a suburban neighborhood. While that might be convenient for people who work

---

7   Pansy Schulman, "Saudi Arabia's The Line Drastically Scales Back Its Ambitions," *Architectural Record RSS*, April 17, 2024, https://www.architecturalrecord.com/articles/16851-saudi-arabias-the-line-drastically-scales-back-its-ambitions.

8   Pratyush Sarup, "The Line in Saudi Arabia: What's Going on with NEOM's Futuristic Project? And When Will It Finish?," *AD Middle East*, May 2, 2024, https://www.admiddleeast.com/story/the-line-in-saudi-arabia-whats-going-on-with-neoms-futuristic-project-and-when-will-it-finish.

at the plant, for everyone else it's a nightmare. So in the game (and in life), people move.

This NEOM project has their residential and commercial all built into The Line. But their industrial section is all in the Oxagon. This not only keeps everything separated, but it also makes it nice and easy for all of the complex logistics to work together in harmony.

Looking at pictures of Oxagon is pretty nuts too. True to its name's portmanteau, it is shaped like an octagon with eight sides (although that's a bit debatable, as you'll understand in a second). But part of the shape is on the land, while the rest floats in a body of water. The entire thing is also bisected by a channel made for allowing water transport in and out of Oxagon. And while it's all just renderings right now, it's pretty cool to check out.

Now you might be thinking that while all of this sounds neat, it also doesn't seem like it could be enough. The Line is going to be 106 miles long. Cities are built with industrial areas nearby commercial and residential zones all the time, *SimCity* be damned. So how can they make this singular industrial area work for an entire city?

And that answer is easy. They're rethinking logistics.

Rethinking Logistics

Previously, with integration, if you plugged in two pipes—production lines, methods of transport, etc.—that you knew about into a system, things might be great. But if you found out later that you needed two more, things would go south. And a lot of this stuff happens because of decades of bureaucracy and just this basic idea: "Logistics are complex because they need to be. As a result, only a few people in the world know how to do this."

As politely put as possible, that's crap.

Let's take the ever-controversial Elon Musk as an example. When he looked at auto manufacturing, he felt like things were too complex. There were lots of moving parts that didn't need to be there, not only in the cars but also specifically in the production process.

Why did everything have to be so difficult? Couldn't you make life easier if you just simplified everything?

That's why things changed at Tesla once he purchased the business. He needed to produce a lot of cars much faster than they were already doing, and he needed to make them cheaper too. He also needed to build an infrastructure that supported his electric cars, because back then, that didn't exist. And he needed to keep everything simple.

The results of that experiment are visible in every Tesla you sit in today. Plop yourself down in a Model 3, and you'll notice a lack of physical buttons pretty much everywhere. Instead of a slider for your A/C or a lever for your shifter, those things and so much more are replaced by controls on a touch screen monitor on the dash. Seriously, if you want to move your air vents, you use the touch screen.

Now whether Musk is the Henry Ford of our time is yet to be seen. But let's compare Tesla's success with one of its rivals: Rivian. They make those trucks with the funky headlights and the little cargo compartment between the cab and the bed. They're pretty popular too. And since they start at $79,000 for the R1T,[9] one would think they're doing all right. Actually, no. Turns out that as of February 26, 2024, they're losing $43,000 per vehicle they make.[10]

Tesla certainly has their fair share of problems, but they're not losing the equivalent amount of one Toyota Sienna minivan for every

---

9   "Configurations," Rivian, accessed June 10, 2024, https://rivian.com/configurations/list?SORT=Featured&MODEL=R1T.

10   Charlie Schlenker, "Rivian's Map to Profitability," WGLT, February 26, 2024, https://www.wglt.org/local-news/2024-02-26/rivians-map-to-profitability.

car they make. And again, it's about taking what was the status quo and rethinking how it has to be.

Disrupting the status quo has been the impetus for many businesses over the years. Uber, the ridesharing app, upended the taxi cab industry. DoorDash and Grubhub changed delivery services. Not all of these ideas are profitable, but again, they're ways to think outside of the box and move things forward.

This is what we need to do with logistics, and while it may not all be obvious right now, I think that change is already coming.

The Silent Shift™

I believe a Silent Shift™ is coming. This is not a small change in the status quo but instead a quiet one—where big adjustments are being made in the way we do things, but they're not being announced in flashy press briefings. It's done in the shadows, and when you realize the change is happening, it's already completed.

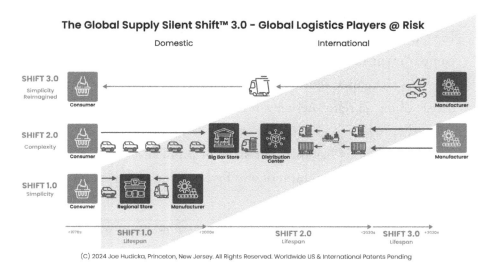

The Global Supply Silent Shift™ 3.0 - Global Logistics Players @ Risk

Let's look at Amazon for a moment. Way back in 2016, they came up with this plan called Operation Dragon Boat.[11] Think about how your Amazon packages used to come to your door. Typically, back then, you would place your order, and in a few days, a UPS, DHL, or FedEx driver would show up with it, ready to go. Have you ever shipped anything via those companies? The cost adds up, and when you're shipping millions of packages a day, that's pricey.

Operation Dragon Boat was designed to eliminate those middlemen. According to the article,

> The goal is to move sellers from booking freight moves with DHL, UPS or FedEx to instead work directly with Amazon, the 2013 plan said. "The ease and transparency of this disintermediation will be revolutionary and sellers will flock to FBA given the competitive pricing."[12]
>
> Amazon will partner with third-party carriers to build the global enterprise and then gradually squeeze them out once the business reaches sufficient volume and Amazon learns enough to run it on its own, Bloomberg reports the documents said. Wow.[13]

That was in 2016. Now let's move forward to 2021. CNBC shared an article titled "Amazon Is Making Its Own Containers and

---

11   Dan Gilmore, "Amazon—The Most Audacious Logistics Plan in History?," *Supply Chain Digest*, February 18, 2016, https://www.scdigest.com/firstthoughts/16-02-18.php?cid=10305.

12   Gilmore, "Amazon."

13   Gilmore, "Amazon."

Bypassing Supply Chain Chaos with Chartered Ships and Long-Haul Planes."[14] (Wow—what a mouthful.)

The article covers how Operation Dragon Boat is chugging right along. They started building their own shipping containers, for one. And if you're in the logistics world, you know all about these things. They can get pricey, and you need them if you want to ship large amounts of goods across the country. So Amazon figured they'd just make their own and not have to pay that extra cost.

But that's not all. They also started rethinking transportation. The article talks about how the port system works. Typically, goods that need to go to California are delivered to Los Angeles at one of their ports. But that means waiting longer to get everything unloaded from the boat and moved forward. If they move that port to Washington state and truck things in, they save time. The article states,

> "Los Angeles, there's 79 vessels sitting out there up to 45 days waiting to come into the harbor," ocean freight analyst Steve Ferreira told CNBC in November. "Amazon's latest venture that I've been tracking in the last two days, it waited two days in the harbor."

So yes, it may cost more to get the products shipped via boat and truck, but how much money are they saving because they're not waiting in a harbor?

Now you need trucks. How does Amazon do that? After all, these aren't just trucks but also drivers, maintenance crews, and all the con-

---

14 Katie Tarasov, "Amazon Is Making Its Own Containers and Bypassing Supply Chain Chaos with Chartered Ships and Long-Haul Planes," CNBC, December 6, 2021, https://www.cnbc.com/2021/12/04/how-amazon-beats-supply-chain-chaos-with-ships-and-long-haul-planes.html.

nective tissue to support everything. Semi drivers need special commercial driver's licenses, or CDLs; otherwise, they can't hit the road. And those kinds of drivers are not as common as you might think.

One solution that they've tendered is the Amazon Freight Partner program.[15] According to their website, the idea is for you, the regular person, to start your own trucking company, and they'll help you get up and running from a logistical perspective. They claim start-up costs can be as low as $40,000 a year, with potential revenue at $1.5–3.5 million a year. That's pretty great.

But let's say you don't want to start a trucking company. What about a delivery center? That's the idea behind Amazon's Delivery Service Partner program (DSP).[16] To quote their website,

> Being a DSP owner is a full-time job. It's a chance for you to open your own business and partner with Amazon. DSPs are heavily involved in their day-to-day operations and are comfortable navigating the ambiguity of a business that changes quickly and frequently. As a DSP, you'll use your passion and work ethic to help Amazon create the future of customer delivery by tackling each day with a sense of purpose and responsibility to your team, customers, and community. You'll have the unique opportunity to create jobs in your neighborhood and lead a team that delivers gifts, textbooks, and pet food to your community.[17]

---

15   "Start Your Trucking Company and Grow with Amazon," Amazon Freight Partner, accessed June 10, 2024, https://freightpartner.amazon.com/marketing/opportunity.

16   "Your Opportunity," Amazon, accessed June 10, 2024, https://logistics.amazon.com/marketing/opportunity.

17   Amazon, "Your Opportunity."

These potential business owners are there to help with what's called "final mile delivery," which is how things get from a warehouse to the customer's front door. Amazon needed a lot of these DSPs set up fast, and establishing a system such as this makes things go even quicker. But you still need trucks to do that job, and that's where things shifted again.

Time was when Amazon relied on USPS, UPS, DHL, and FedEx to get the job done. The problem was not only the cost but also a lack of control. And so in 2019 they decided to shift everything under their own roof.[18]

Now to do this, you need trucks. And anecdotally, I can say that at least some of the trucks looked like reskinned and wrapped retired UPS vehicles. But they connected with Rivian, a then virtually unheard-of electric car company, with the goal of putting one hundred thousand electric trucks on the road by 2030.[19] That exclusive electric vehicle deal ended in November 2023, but the two companies are still working together, and the fleet is expanding even further. All of those trucks go to DSPs, by the way.

Is that even enough? I don't know about you, but I see a lot of Amazon packages sitting on my neighbors' porches. And sometimes two-day delivery isn't fast enough. How could they get things to customers' doorsteps in even less time?

Well, one option that I've seen is Amazon Flex.[20] You know how Uber is a ridesharing program where a person uses their personal

---

18 Warren Shoulberg, "5 Reasons Amazon May Be Going Too Far by Taking Over Its Own Deliveries," *Forbes*, last updated October 1, 2019, https://www.forbes.com/sites/warrenshoulberg/2019/09/25/5-reasons-why-amazon-may-be-going-too-far-by-taking-over-its-own-deliveries/?sh=84474c148701.

19 "Rivian to End Exclusivity with Amazon, Allow Other Companies to Buy Its Electric Vans," Associated Press, last updated November 7, 2023, https://apnews.com/article/rivian-ev-amazon-delivery-f9168099d0f911b479845722d5e22b2d.

20 "Amazon Flex—US," Amazon Flex, accessed June 11, 2024, https://flex.amazon.com/.

vehicle like a taxi and takes strangers for rides in exchange for funds. Now swap "strangers" with "packages," and you've got the basic idea behind Amazon Flex. Gig workers load up their cars with a bunch of packages and then deliver them to people.

Could you imagine any of those scenarios happening even ten years ago? That a company as large as Amazon would shift all of their deliveries to their own trucks and a version of Uber for packages? No, and that's part of the genius of the whole thing. They didn't make a big, flashy statement to the world about it. Instead, they slowly and quietly built this all up to the point where now they have multiple options for every package to start in one part of the world and end up in another in very short order.

That's the thing about the Silent Shift™: it's not a small change, but nobody believes it's going to happen until it's too late for them to react.

The China Component

Now you probably know that China plays an outsize role in everything involving shipping. And for years, they put everything on container ships and sent them out to sea. It was the easiest way to get things around the world, after all. But really, was it? They wanted to rethink things as well.

That's why during the pandemic, they took a stretch of railroad and turned a previously low-use method of transportation into a flourishing option.[21]

21   Yaku Fumie et al., "Pandemic Turns 'Iron Silk Road' into China-Europe Trade Artery," Nikkei Asia, June 11, 2021, https://asia.nikkei.com/Spotlight/Belt-and-Road/Pandemic-turns-Iron-Silk-Road-into-China-Europe-trade-artery.

Sea transportation did make a lot of sense, as did air. If you've ever ordered a laptop from Apple that wasn't in stock locally, you know that it flies over the ocean to get to you. Similar things happen in Europe as well. Thing is, there weren't a lot of pilots doing their jobs during the pandemic, and there had to be some way to get goods from China to Europe, and this railroad was it. They'd pile goods onto a car, then send it off. Just that easy.

This is also part of a Chinese initiative first heard of in 2013 called the Belt and Road Initiative, or, as it's known in China, the One Belt One Road.[22] The idea was for China to build out a global infrastructure in over 150 countries and international organizations. They're all connected logistically, including energy, ports, digital infrastructure, and ground transportation. It's a pretty huge deal.

Already, this initiative is getting pretty close to the finish line. As of this writing, they're in over 140 countries that make up two-thirds of the world's population.[23] Their goal is to have the Belt and Road Initiative done by 2049,[24] which, were they not already in 140 countries now, would seem about right. But now? Well, that seems way too far off.

This is all about their rethinking of how things are done. Planes aren't working? Let's fire up the trains. Can't get goods to one area? Let's build roads there for them to get everything transported faster. It's a completely audacious and aspirational plan on its face, and yet here we are, seeing that they're already very far down the, ahem, road.

---

22 James McBride et al., "China's Massive Belt and Road Initiative," Council on Foreign Relations, last updated February 2, 2023, https://www.cfr.org/backgrounder/chinas-massive-belt-and-road-initiative.

23 McBride et al., "China's Massive Belt and Road Initiative."

24 Samuel Powers, "CrowdReviews Partnered with Strategic Marketing & Exhibitions to Announce: One Belt, One Road Forum," PR.com, March 25, 2019, https://www.pr.com/press-release/780645.

A Change Is Gonna Come

Whether it's the Silent Shift™, the development of Belt and Road Initiative, or the Oxagon, people are rethinking how the logistics industry is functioning. This is going to radically change how people get things shipped, and if you're not on the train, you'd better board fast. This is going to happen with or without you.

But if there's one thing that's constant, it's change. There will be more adjustments to the way work is done. People will find new pathways, new efficiencies, and different methods to improve the system. And from my perspective, I think a lot of that is going to include AI and less friction.

We have to stop building these software silos and start building secure ecosystems. If we don't, those efficiencies will never be as realized as they could be.

That is, of course, the whole point of the book. But let me state it right here: it's time for you and your company to step up so you're not left behind. As the song says, a change is gonna come.

CHAPTER TWO

Assess Negotiation

But if you try sometimes,
Well, you just might find
You get what you need.

—"YOU CAN'T ALWAYS GET WHAT YOU WANT," THE ROLLING STONES

It's impossible to get an accurate view of where you're going without first assessing where you are. And right now, that's a pretty tough thing to do.

Let's start by talking about negotiation. There are plenty of times when you have to go into a boardroom somewhere or get on a call and hammer out the pricing. Thing is, you're not always talking to a person. As it turns out, humans aren't the only ones working on pricing information—bots are too.

AI and the bots that came before them are changing how we do business in pretty much every field. These automated systems can go out and look for prices that are available publicly and then give you the data you need to outbid your competition.

The problem is that now bots and AI are competing against each other. Your team has those resources, as does the competition, and so do other parties that may or may not be involved. How can you win a quote against a bot? They're faster to win the deal and secure the load or capacity you may need for your next shipment. How do you make that work?

Then there's e-commerce and its impact on the market. They have these giant companies that have portals that allow people to completely bypass the traditional pallet consolidation model. And that's nuts.

Flying Fast Fashion

Now in the last chapter, I talked about Amazon—how they decided to take over their entire supply flow from soup to nuts and make sure they were the folks who handled all of their packages. This meant getting their own trucks, cargo containers, and a ton more, all through Operation Dragon Boat. It's crazy stuff.

And yet when one door closes, another one opens—right? Amazon decides their solution involves building massive distribution centers, shipping their own cargo containers on their own boats, and delivering them to those distribution centers on their trucks with their own smaller trucks and gig workers handling the last mile. And right there appears an opening: What about planes?

Now this is a complex topic, but fortunately, I know a guy. His name is Jordan Frohlinger, but I know him as Jordan Frohlinger, global airline/air freight executive, e-commerce and project logistics

SME, freight expert, and supply chain consultant. Actually, I'll just let him introduce himself.

> Sure. I've been an air guy my entire career. I've been through three airlines, both passenger and freight. I started my career off at Spirit, managing operations. Then I moved on to Atlas Air, which is how Joe and I know each other.

Atlas Air, by the way, is the fifth-biggest cargo airline by fleet size,[25] and it's the largest operator of Boeing 747s. To get into the specifics, Jordan elaborated, "Atlas Air is an airline primarily designed to subcontract for carriers looking to supplement their freight or passenger fleet."

Between his current position and the years of experience that he has in the industry, he's a pretty big expert in the field. And boy oh boy does he know a lot about how fast fashion plays into the air cargo game.

Wait. Fast fashion? What's that?

Take your Gap, your Adidas, and your Levi's. These companies make clothing all over the world, and some, if not most, of their products come from overseas.

Jordan explained, "Clothing's being made, manufactured in Vietnam or China and then being shipped over by boat." Then it comes into the country and is sent out to distribution centers, which then send them directly to consumers and retail stores.

---

25   Vincenzo Claudio Piscopo, "These Are the 5 Biggest Cargo Airlines Worldwide by Fleet Size," Simple Flying, January 20, 2024, https://simpleflying.com/biggest-cargo-fleets-list/#:~:text=FedEx%20Express%2C%20a%20subsidiary%20of,an%20additional%2063%20new%20planes.

"They keep costs down, and that's a large segment of the market, but it's not the cutting edge."

You know what that is? Slow. And we're talking about fashion here, folks. When you see a celebrity wearing a killer outfit online and you want one to match, you want it now. You're going to memory hole the whole thing if you wait a couple of days, so speed is of utmost importance.

Enter fast fashion. The idea here is to produce goods cheaply overseas and then ship them in bulk via air cargo to their destination. There are no distribution centers, no cargo containers to unload, and no speed bumps along the way. The fashion gets to the customer faster. Hence the name.

One of Atlas's big customers is Inditex.[26] They own a lot of fast fashion companies with brands such as Zara under their masthead. "Fast fashion has been moving goods by air freight since the late '90s. Atlas became a beneficiary later as the industry grew and Inditex sourced their own controlled capacity," Jordan said.

As you could probably guess, air cargo has been an expensive way to get something fast. It's also a way to get your laptop to you as quickly as possible, without the long lines and time crunches associated with ocean freight. So on the surface, that would seem like a really expensive way for fast fashion to get delivered to their customers, particularly when it's sold so cheap. But as it turns out, there's a few good reasons why.

Let's start with something kind of technical. You're probably familiar with the de minimis tax exemption, right? If not, here's the basics. As they put it on the National Foreign Trade Council's website:

---

26 "Inditex Homepage," Inditex, accessed June 11, 2024, https://www.inditex.com/itxcomweb/en/home.

The De Minimis Tax Exemption is a law that Congress passed on a bipartisan basis that allows shipments bound for American businesses and consumers valued under $800 (per person, per day) to enter the U.S. free of duty and taxes.[27]

"Fast fashion, electronics, and all goods can benefit from the de minimis tax exemption that allows articles to be free of import duty for items that do not exceed $800, which is why Chinese e-commerce companies are now direct-to-consumer. There are no duties, and the air freight is much cheaper rather than mass shipping products to the US and storing them in US warehouses until someone buys the goods," Jordan said.

Per the National Foreign Trade Council, "While the tax exemption allows for tax-free treatment, U.S. Customs and Border Protection (CBP) screens these low-value shipments just as they would screen higher-value entries coming through other modes. These shipments are subject to screening and review by over fifty federal agencies enforcing over 500 U.S. laws."[28]

What that means is that your iPhone or MacBook comes into the country, and you have to pay duty and taxes, but products less than $800 per unit,[29] such as fast fashion clothing items, are exempt.

Ever heard of Shein? They're one of the many brands out there under the fast fashion category, and either you or someone you know

---

27 "De Minimis: A Vital Tax Exemption," National Foreign Trade Council, accessed June 6, 2024, https://www.nftc.org/de-minimis-a-vital-tax-exemption/#:~:text=What%20 is%20the%20De%20Minimis,free%20of%20duty%20and%20taxes.

28 "De Minimis: A Vital Tax Exemption," National Foreign Trade Council, accessed September 13, 2024, https://www.nftc.org/de-minimis-a-vital-tax-exemption/.

29 National Foreign Trade Council, "De Minimis: A Vital Tax Exemption."

has ordered from them before, or you've heard of them through social media. This stuff is cheap, and it's all shipped via air.

I decided to confirm this before I went ahead and wrote the whole thing down, so let me throw out an example. I found an item—SHEIN EZwear Letter Graphic Thermal Lined Sweatshirt[30]—and it was $9.29, a 12 percent markdown from the original price of $10.59. It's a sweatshirt, it's orange (although they have other choices), and it says "Miami Florida" across the front with a little flower in the middle. It's cute, and at under $10.00, it's almost criminally cheap.

To compare, I went to Target's website and found this—Women's Beautifully Soft Fleece Sweatshirt—Stars Above™[31]—for $19.99. It's not the same color, nor does it have the print on the front. But it looks to be a similar material and quality. It's double the price of the Shein item, and while I might be able to get it in store, I can have it shipped, which will take about a week to get to me. If I get two shirts, I can have it shipped for free.

Shein's shipping on that item? A little bit longer at ten days, but it's half the price. And if I spend $29, I get shipping for free. Of course, that's three shirts, not two. And while it may take me a little bit longer on this particular order, I'll get more for my money. Sold.

So how do they do this? First, almost all of their products fall into the de minimis tax exemption. Point is, the bulk of their items don't get taxed, so that's some savings on their end. The goods themselves

---

30 "Shein EZwear Letter Graphic Thermal Lined Sweatshirt," SHEIN, accessed June 11, 2024, https://us.shein.com/SHEIN-EZwear-Letter-Graphic-Thermal-Lined-Sweatshirt-p-15344926.html?src_identifier=on%3DIMAGE_COMPONENT%60 cn%3Dshopbycate%60hz%3DhotZone_1%60ps%3D2_1%60jc%3Dreal_2030& src_module=All&src_tab_page_id=page_home1714757826971&mallCode=1&pageLi stType=4&imgRatio=3-4.

31 "Women's Beautifully Soft Fleece Sweatshirt—Stars Above™," Target, accessed June 11, 2024, https://www.target.com/p/women-s-beautifully-soft-fleece-sweatshirt-stars-above/-/A-81305860?preselect=89653542#lnk=same tab.

are made overseas, which means they're done inexpensively, and since they're fabric, they pack into nice and small packages. Oh, and usually, they're light boxes too.

But still, if Gap and everyone else are following the same protocols, how is this better?

Well, let's get into the "fast" part of fast fashion. If a designer for Gap comes up with an idea, they have to design it, send it to their shops overseas, have them make it, and then it gets shipped back to the States in a process that could take weeks. Shein does all that but sends it via air cargo, which means that trendy item goes from their production facility to customer's hands super quick. And one other thing. There are no distribution centers; they just pack them up and ship their wares directly to the consumer.

Isn't air cargo expensive? It certainly can be, but Shein can pack hundreds of orders into a freight plane. But how? The *how* can be a little bit more complicated.

Let's say that you're a shipping company, and you need to send things via air cargo. To do that, you sign a yearlong lease that says you're going to use X amount of space on the plane. Well, what if you don't end up needing all that space? You're still paying for it, so is there a better way to make up this loss?

"Shein/Temu (and parent company PDD Holdings) are all procuring their own controlled capacity in order to fulfill orders in every way possible," Jordan said. "They are shopping wisely by buying controlled capacity from the market and other beneficial owners who are turning around and selling it to Shein/Temu to take it off their hands or even to make a profit from."

Companies such as Shein will get their products to the States and other countries super quickly, and they don't have to worry about taxes because of de minimis. They save money on the goods, the overhead associated with distribution centers, and time with transportation because they ship off the plane with FedEx, DHL, and UPS. And chances are, you paid the actual cost of shipping either by purchasing more goods than you would have normally or just paying outright.

Seriously, these fast fashion folks are printing money. Air cargo is no big deal for them. And guess what. They're not the only ones who are doing it.

Let's Talk Planes and DTC

Between Shein and Temu, about six thousand packages a day come across the ocean on air cargo[32] according to an early 2024 article in Reuters. If you want even more fun math, check out this quote:

> According to data aggregated by Cargo Facts Consulting, Temu ships around 4,000 tonnes a day, Shein 5,000 tonnes, Alibaba.com 1,000 tonnes and TikTok 800 tonnes. That equates to around 108 Boeing 777 freighters a day, the consultancy said.[33]

Here's another goodie. According to the House Select Committee on the Chinese Communist Party, 30 percent of all packages valued

---

32   Arriana McLymore et al., "Focus: Rise of Fast-Fashion Shein, Temu Roils Global Air Cargo Industry," Reuters, April 10, 2024, https://www.reuters.com/business/retail-consumer/rise-fast-fashion-shein-temu-roils-global-air-cargo-industry-2024-02-21/.

33   McLymore et al., "Focus."

under $800 (and therefore hit the de minimis exception) in 2022 were shipped from Shein and Temu.[34]

I've already thrown out there a few reasons why companies such as Shein and Temu are pushing things via air instead of boat, but there are other factors as well. One of the bigger ones is the Red Sea. If you've got a cargo vessel and you want to run through the Suez Canal, you're going to get into the Red Sea either coming or going. The problem is that the Houthis are attacking ships in the Red Sea, which is causing delays and potential losses.[35] The only other alternative from a boat perspective is going all the way around Africa, and that will take you quite a bit longer. And time is money, people.

Another big impact was the rise of the direct-to-consumer (DTC) market. Jordan has seen this happen firsthand. "The world is changing to direct-to-consumer and direct from the manufacturer, which is saving costs and making products less expensive for consumers. As a consequence, there are significantly more items moving through air freight channels and consuming global capacity."

The Middleman Shift

I remember that I used to love coming to New York City when I needed to go get nice, new business attire. For that, I went to a store named Barneys. It had some nostalgia to it. You could walk in and find all of the crazy brands that you wanted to see. And if you needed

34   "Fast Fashion and the Uyghur Genocide: Interim Findings," Select Committee on the Chinese Communist Party, accessed June 11, 2024, https://selectcommitteeontheccp. house.gov/sites/evo-subsites/selectcommitteeontheccp.house.gov/files/evo-media-document/fast-fashion-and-the-uyghur-genocide-interim-findings.pdf.

35   Richa Naidu, "Walmart and Adidas Cargo Aboard, One Ship's Voyage to Avoid the Red Sea," Reuters, January 31, 2024, https://www.reuters.com/business/retail-consumer/walmart-adidas-cargo-aboard-one-ships-voyage-avoid-red-sea-2024-01-31/.

a little quiet time, they had a little restaurant where you could relax. It was great.

Barneys, as a physical location independent of any others, is dead.[36] They got bought by Authentic Brands Group in 2020, and now they're licensed out to Saks Fifth Avenue as a specialty department within those stores.

But you don't have to believe me. Just head down to your local mall—assuming it still exists. The kinds of places that you used to go have fun when you were a kid (or at least when I was a kid) are gone.

Way back in the introduction, I explained how a seminal part of my childhood was the experience of getting the one-inch thick Sears toy catalog before Christmas every year. I would flip through that thing for hours, circling what I wanted and hoping something would end up under the tree. But now Sears is pretty much gone, with only ten stores left as of April 2024.[37] No more catalogs.

They're not the only ones. Circuit City wasn't cheap, but if I wanted to buy some home audio equipment or get a new car stereo, they were the spot. I can't go there anymore.[38] My mom used to shop at Filene's, a department store chain founded in 1881. They shut down in 2006.[39] And you'll never find this book at Waldenbooks, because

36   Danny Parisi, "The End of the Department Store Era," Glossy, November 19, 2021, https://www.glossy.co/fashion/the-end-of-the-department-store-era/.

37   Jordan Valinsky, "The Last Sears in the New York Area Is Closing. Just Over a Dozen Remain in America," CNN, January 11, 2024, https://www.cnn.com/2024/01/11/business/sears-new-jersey-location-closing/index.html.

38   Jessie Romero, "The Rise and Fall of Circuit City," Economic History, 2013, https://www.richmondfed.org/publications/research/econ_focus/2013/q3/~/media/4EDF64C581574974B9AAE6B3D7C88A9A.ashx.

39   "Research Guides: Filene's Department Store History and Marketing Archives: Home," n.d., https://guides.bpl.org/filenes.

they were bought by Kmart, then spun off after being combined with Borders, which then failed in 2011.[40]

So why does all this matter? Does it matter at all? Well, all of those big stores that existed, plus the ones that still do, are middlemen. They're the folks who buy the goods from the supplier then sell them off to their customers.

Today, middlemen are disappearing, and at first you might think that was a good thing. No more paying those fat cats your hard-earned cash, right? But DTC sellers often don't have storefronts. There's no way for you to browse the aisles in the physical world to see what you like. Is that fabric of a good quality? You'll have a better idea if you're touching it in a store versus scrolling on your laptop.

Think about Amazon. There was a time when they opened physical stores to sell their goods, such as Amazon Books, Amazon Go, and Amazon Fresh. Well, Amazon Books is gone as of 2022,[41] and they're taking down Amazon Go and Amazon Fresh stores too.[42] And did you even know that Amazon Style existed? I didn't, but it doesn't matter, because they've been eighty-sixed now as well.[43] Even Amazon, the middleman of all middlemen, is a victim to the Silent Shift™.

---

40   Áine Cain, "4 Once-Beloved Booksellers That Have Closed Their Doors for Good," *Business Insider*, October 6, 2019, https://www.businessinsider.com/bookstores-closed-borders-bookstop-waldenbooks-2019-10.

41   Jeffrey Dastin, "Amazon to Shut Its Bookstores and Other Shops as Its Grocery Chain Expands," Reuters, March 2, 2022, https://www.reuters.com/business/retail-consumer/exclusive-amazon-close-all-its-physical-bookstores-4-star-shops-2022-03-02/.

42   Walter Loeb, "Amazon Is Closing Some Amazon Fresh and Amazon Go Stores—Are Groceries Profitable?," *Forbes*, February 13, 2023, https://www.forbes.com/sites/walterloeb/2023/02/10/amazon-is-closing-some-amazon-fresh-and-amazon-go-stores--are-groceries-profitable/.

43   Haleluya Hadero, "Amazon Closing Two Clothing Stores in Another Failed Bid into Physical Retail," Associated Press, last updated November 2, 2023, https://apnews.com/article/amazon-style-stores-closed-71e4d0fecaff4a0a56b193e50fae0c35.

Say I've got a company named Joe Knows Clothes. (I know, it's a refreshing name.) My business is selling T-shirts to big retail stores. Now technically, do I care what you, the average person, wants? Not really. If the retail stores want it, that's good enough for me. Does it bother me if the store never sells a single unit? Nope. I got my money, so that's that.

But now, today, particularly with the fast fashion brands that I've talked about all chapter, the shift is toward DTC—direct-to-consumer. Now I *do* care about what the end user wants, because they're my customer. It makes me more responsive to changes in the market and keeps me on my toes. And for the purposes of this book, it also adjusts how I handle my logistics. If speed is a priority, then I need to get those clothes on planes and adjust my costs accordingly.

Of course, that also sounds like a lot of complex math. I wonder if there's some kind of way that you could automate all that and intelligently come up with methods for improving everything.

AI and Logistics

Today, as it stands, logistics are a cost center. We have to do that complex math, hire people to coordinate things, and make sure everyone gets their widgets on time. We don't love it, but it is what it is. There's no way that's going to change, right?

Ah, but maybe we can. Instead of looking at logistics as a cost center, let's pivot and make them a way to grow a profitable business. And we do that through lots and lots of fancy tools, including spreadsheets, tons of data, and AI.

I haven't talked a lot about AI and its use in the industry yet, but let me take a brief beat to lay that out. AI, as we understand it from the movies, stands for artificial intelligence. You may have seen the 2001 movie *A.I.* by Steven Spielberg, or possibly you're thinking about *I, Robot* with Will Smith. Either way, that ain't how AI works today, so let's get into it.

Today's AI is really called generative AI.[44] To dumb it down incredibly, these generative AI models take in data and then use that information to make predictions. If you ask an AI model such as ChatGPT what the weather is like historically in Florida during the summer, it will comb its data set and answer the question with predictive text. Basically, the AI will start with the most likely word to form a response, then follow that with the next most likely word to follow the first, and so on. So it's not *real* artificial intelligence in the movie sense. (In fact, that's now called AGI, which is artificial general intelligence, but that's a whole other book.)

Now this is a neat parlor trick, but what can it do for logistics? Well, what today's AI is really good at is taking in data and then extracting results from it.

Let's say that your shipping company has been around for twenty-five years, which means you have twenty-five years of data. You can also find more data around things such as weather, general climate conditions, or what kind of world conflicts there were over those twenty-five years. Now you feed all that into a generative AI system, and with that information you can ask it questions—normal, human questions, not something you have to say like a robot.

What kind of questions? Things such as "Based on the history of my company, what do you expect will be the flow of products coming through my business in May 2025?" That's information that, if it has the right data, an AI system could suss out.

---

44   Kesha Williams, "What Are Transformers in Generative AI?," Pluralsight, April 15, 2024, https://www.pluralsight.com/resources/blog/data/what-are-transformers-generative-ai.

Now let's put that into the logistics equation. You can feed all of your customer profiles into a private AI system, which gives it more data to work from. We could take that information, plus everything else the AI has gobbled up, to optimize volume throughput. What does that do for you? Well, it helps stabilize pricing, and it maximizes profitability. That's not too shabby right there, and it could change the way you do business. You go from a static price book model to a dynamic revenue management model, and now you're driving and balancing demand to meet capacity. How's that for some efficiency?

AI is just one of these tools that you can have on hand to move your business forward. And just wait, because you're going to hear about it plenty more.

You Can't Always Get What You Want

Now this trend of using air over boats may not last forever. It's not cheap, and there are environmental concerns to think about as well. But for now, just take those thoughts and set them to the side. What you should think about here is how these companies are taking a different approach from the status quo. And that is key.

Let's go back to the desert for a second and compare the air cargo issue with the Oxagon. They decided to transform the entire logistics experience from soup to nuts. Are Shein, Temu, and Alibaba doing the same thing? Well, they're certainly going outside the realm of traditional thinking, and that's the takeaway. You have to think outside of the box with your logistics, or else you will get left behind.

And to do that, you have to assess where you are today and start to postulate on where you're going to be in the future. Look, that's really hard to do. That's why tools like AI will help you figure out some of the mess we're in today and how to sort it out for the future.

But there is a missing component here to move you forward. AI doesn't work unless it's fed a solid diet of data—and good data too. Once you have the ability to get some good information fed into your system, then you can really start to move toward the future.

Here's the thing: You can't always get what you want. But if you try sometimes, you just might find, you get what you need.

CHAPTER THREE

Analyze Performance

I can still hear you saying
You would never break the chain
(Never break the chain)

—"THE CHAIN," FLEETWOOD MAC

There's a movie that I've thought about a lot recently. It's the 2011 film *Moneyball* with Brad Pitt, and it tells the story of Billy Beane, the one-time player turned GM for the Oakland Athletics. It's based on the book *Moneyball: The Art of Winning an Unfair Game* by Michael Lewis, and without any spoilers, what Billy Beane did changed the way baseball was played for years.

Baseball has always been a statistics-driven sport. Go to any stadium in the country, and you'll see some old-timers out there with a scoring sheet and a tiny pencil, recording every hit, error, and bunt along the way. You don't see that during football games, that's for sure. So it's natural that someone would come along and figure out a way to use those stats to figure out how to play the game better. While baseball isn't a game of inches, it is one of numbers.

Enter Earnshaw Cook, the author of *Percentage Baseball*. He was one of the first people to employ the empirical analysis of baseball known as sabermetrics.[45] Then in 1977, Bill James's book, *The Bill James Historical Baseball Abstract*, came out, which assembled annual baseball data into one document. This information began to cut at the core of what baseball was, at least to the people who followed the logic of sabermetrics.

See, back then, everyone looked at a player's batting average, which divides a player's hits by times at bat. But that really wasn't what these statisticians thought you should consider. Instead, *scoring* was what was important. Who cares if you could hit if you didn't score?

Now let's get back to Beane. With the help of his assistant, Paul DePodesta, they created a system where the goal was to get the player on base. Not hit a home run, not score, not bunt. Get on base. Because they knew, statistically, following the logic of sabermetrics, that if their players got on base, they were in a better position to score. Players who did so scored more often, and they didn't need to be a big-name player. They could create a team for very little money who could hold strong against the larger clubs. And they did it using a decades-old book that had been largely ignored.

Now spoiler for a movie that's a decade or so old, but the Oakland A's didn't win the World Series that season, and Beane almost got hired away by the Boston Red Sox. Beane would later famously say to the author of *Moneyball*, Michael Lewis, "My shit doesn't work in

---

45   "A Guide to Sabermetric Research," Society for American Baseball Research, n.d., https://sabr.org/sabermetrics.

the playoffs,"[46] and it didn't—at least not for him. In 2004, just two years or so after the *Moneyball* season of 2002, the Boston Red Sox would win their first World Series in eighty-six years. And they did it using Beane's techniques. (To add insult to injury, they did it with an ex-member of the Oakland A's, Johnny Damon.)

So why am I rambling on about baseball when I'm really more of a movie guy? Because what Beane and the A's did for baseball, we can do for logistics. We just need to start looking at the analytics.

The Bullwhip Effect

We in the logistics industry base a lot of our decisions on predictions. The assumption is that what has happened in the past will happen in the present day, and therefore, we should accommodate things from a workflow perspective using that information. We don't lean into things such as predictive weather patterns or data that comes from potential disruptions. Instead, we say, "Well, it happened this way last year, so let's roll the dice on this one."

One of the problems with this system comes when things really hit the fan. Like, say, when a global pandemic throws the emergency brake on the global economy, and we're all trying to find a way to buy toilet paper.

Now you probably know all about the bullwhip effect, but just in case, let's walk it through. I find these kinds of things easier to visualize, so take a peep at this:

---

46   Tim Keown, "Billy Beane's Grand Experiment," ESPN, September 4, 2014, https://www.espn.com/mlb/story/_/id/11426305/ oakland-billy-beane-talks-wheeling-dealing-team-playoff-hopes.

The Bullwhip's Effect on Profit and Loss

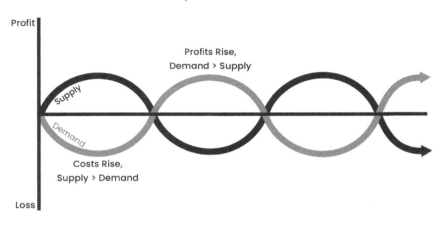

What we've got here looks a bit like a sine wave, and it has its similarities. Let's go to the Chartered Institute of Procurement & Supply, or CIPS, to see what they say about the bullwhip effect:

> The bullwhip effect is the demand distortion that travels upstream in the supply chain. Upstream in the supply chain consists of the retailer through to the wholesaler and manufacture. The distortion is created by the variance of orders which may be larger than sales.[47]

But Investopedia makes it a bit more clear:

---

[47] "Bullwhip Effect in Supply Chains," CIPS, accessed June 11, 2024, https://www.cips. org/intelligence-hub/operations-management/bullwhip-effect.

The bullwhip effect refers to a scenario in which small changes in demand at the retail end of the supply chain become amplified when moving up the supply chain from the retail end to the manufacturing end.

This happens when a retailer changes how much of a good it orders from wholesalers based on a small change in real or predicted demand for that good. Due to not having full information on the demand shift, the wholesaler will increase its orders from the manufacturer by an even larger extent, and the manufacturer, being even more removed will change its production by a still larger amount.[48]

So like a bullwhip, the wave created starts off as small but then gets substantially bigger by the time it hits the end.

Let's put this into context by taking you back to the halcyon days of March 2020 (sarcasm very much intended). Everyone was told to stay home. The idea was we couldn't leave the house, and if we all stayed still, we could knock this new "coronavirus" out forever. Spoiler: That didn't happen.

But what did happen was when we all did go back out into the wild, we saw a lot of empty shelves and missing goods, which made sense because there was nobody to restock items, nobody to order them, no one to load them on a truck, etc.

If you've ever spent time in the Northeastern United States, you've seen this before. The media reports a pending snowstorm, people

---

48   Nathan Reiff, "Bullwhip Effect: Meaning, Example, Impact," Investo-
       pedia, last updated May 3, 2024, https://www.investopedia.com/
       bullwhip-effect-definition-5499228.

flock to their local markets and clean the place out, overstocking on essentials "just in case." Then when you, the person who just needs to get the basics for a regular trip, visit the store, the shelves are empty.

All this happened worldwide, simultaneously, in stores everywhere.

Let me tell you a quick story. My dad used to do his shopping by scouring the papers for the best coupons he could find at any one of the five stores in one of the three nearby towns. He'd only buy the best deals from each. Were you to walk downstairs to his basement, you'd find dozens of bottles of bleach, cases of canned food, and an entire upright freezer filled to the brim. Turns out my dad was running his own warehouse.

So when the pandemic happened, my dad looked like the trend-setter who was ahead of the curve—a man, yet again, ahead of his time. But now there were millions of people doing the same thing as him, which meant retailers weren't able to keep up with the unprecedented demand. They started to signal their supply partners and distribution centers to stock up. That led procurement to request more goods from wholesalers, who would alert their suppliers, who would then sort things out with their transportation and logistics partners. There was positive demand everywhere, more so than ever before.

Now can you see how the bullwhip effect worked here?

Outside demand is always met with a shortfall of supply—and why not? Why would any link of your proverbial supply chain stock up with more materials or finished goods than they believe the next link in their chain will buy? It's all very logical. It makes sense.

But when those excessive demand signals are heard over a long enough period of time, supply signals begin to change too. Suppliers see an opportunity for not only increased sales but also maybe even a lift in price due to the market imbalance of supply being short of demand. As a result, suppliers invest in producing greater supply, and within a short amount of time, store shelves are stocked full again.

Good news, right? Except now the pendulum swings the other direction. Panic shopping decreases, which reduces demand, and now shifts the problem to supply. They've got too much stuff, and when suppliers sit on massive inventories, that's not good either.

Well, I suppose the good news is that things don't get any more complicated, right?

Right?

Things Get More Complicated

Yeah, sorry, but things do get worse.

Let's go back to the Silent Shift™ concept. These are the things that shuffle around in the night that change the direction a company is moving, a product is being logistically handled, or whatever the case may be. It happens away from public eyes, but this mammoth change in the way things are done happens, and we all have to take notice.

So back when Amazon did their Silent Shift™, when they took over their own logistics from FedEx and UPS, there was a void. All of a sudden, UPS, FedEx, and, to a lesser extent, USPS, found themselves with less things to ship and the capacity to take on more work. A few years later, the direct-to-consumer market filled it, partially because of the convenience of shopping from home. The pandemic hits, and brands such as Temu and Shein, which we discussed in the last chapter, do their own Silent Shift™, becoming dominant in the air freight industry and quietly taking over the fast fashion market.

Where does that put us? Well, at this point, cargo isn't in big consolidated containers the way it was before, moving through seaports to distribution centers to stores. That means the ports are just a little bit more empty. That's a temporary thing, right?

Well, sure, maybe. But what about the cost of those distribution centers? The staff, rent, equipment, utilities, and property taxes—where does all that go?

And this is where we bump up against the Silent Shift™ again. These shifts are like the dark matter of the universe. They're invisible forces that do exist but appear unreal at first and harmless at best—until logos start to disappear.

Once a Silent Shift™ happens, somebody is going to feel that pinch. One could make the argument that UPS or FedEx could've gone down once Amazon pulled most of their business. And it's possible that businesses connected to UPS and FedEx did close their doors because they were filling in gaps for the big shippers that no longer needed to be filled.

And what about small shippers? I have a buddy who is a local delivery guy in the Chicago area. He's an individual contractor. He'll go out in his van that he purchased with his own money, drive an hour to downtown, and then spend the rest of his day pushing boxes. He does small-time jobs. What happens when that business dries up because someone else does their own Silent Shift™?

These complications and movements make things like the bullwhip effect really difficult to manage. On the one hand, everyone's gotta eat. But on the other, if we all don't get more efficient, we're all going to starve.

I remember back in the late 1990s when I visited one of my greatest inspirations and mentors, the late Clayton Christensen. His book, *The Innovator's Dilemma,* had just come out, and I was in Cambridge to do some business and say hi. One of the things we talked about was how all of these things—the auto industry collapse and the venture capital industry—that he predicted had come to be but weren't yet visible to the world. We didn't have the Silent Shift™ term yet, but there it was, happening all around us. But nobody was listening.

And yet there needs to be another shift. One that makes things less complicated. Right now, we're in the efficiency stage. What we need to do next is go to collaboration.

Why Can't We Be Friends?

You might think that we in the logistics industry have efficiency down pat. After all, we get our packages (mostly) on time, so it's all good. Except, yeah, it isn't.

If we were efficient, we probably wouldn't have this mammoth series of levels to our flow, which requires this virtual ball to be handed from one to the other down the line. It's like a big game of Telephone but with boxes. It works, sure. But a broken clock is right twice a day, and nobody would ever say that was the most efficient way to tell time.

Let's throw this into an example by going back to Joe Knows Clothes, my clothing store from chapter 2. Imagine I discovered that I'm running low on these fancy designer socks that my customers love. They prevent odors, they never fall down, and they look good. Perfect socks.

Well, I need to order some, so I call my supplier. He takes my order, and then he has to get them in stock too. That means another phone call or email—and if you think my supplier goes direct to the source, you're probably wrong. There are layers upon layers of contacts that have to be made before the company that *actually* manufacturers the socks can get to work. And that means there are a lot of potential miscommunication problems.

All it takes is for one person to say the wrong thing in an email or on a call and the socks I ordered in white are now actually black. Or, even worse, my package with the *right* socks gets lost in the system, because somebody mistyped a tracking number or address because it was obfuscated or entered incorrectly somewhere down the chain. Again, it's the game of Telephone, and it's the way we work through the global supply chain.

Where's My Stuff?
Each Step of the Supply Chain Is Another Opportunity for a Package to Be LOST!

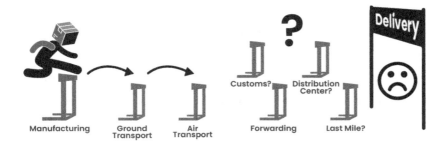

What we need to do is move from efficiency to collaboration. Now that's just step one, but it's a big deal. Here's why.

The shipping and logistics industry is huge. It's how everyone everywhere gets everything they've ever needed. While there is communication among people at each link of the supply chain, there isn't *collaboration*. We're working together but not *together*.

The difference, really, is sharing. As they said to me as a kid, sharing is caring, and we need that to happen. What should we share? Data.

It's obvious why we're not sharing data, and there are probably a million reasons why. Maybe it's proprietary, so you feel like you have a copyright on that information. Or it's formatted weird, so it doesn't sync up with mine. Say it's your secret, and that's the way you make money. Look, I get it. You've got your data, and there's no way you want to share it with everyone.

But think about this: What if you did? What if you shared data with just one other person in the chain? Maybe even a competitor? Would everything stop functioning and you lose your company? Or would things get better for both of you?

I understand you have fears, and I know that because I've thought about all of them, such as the following:

- My partners will overcharge me if they know what my real volume is or will be.

- I get the best pricing when my partners all think they can win more of my volume.

- My competitors will try to steal my capacity allocations if they know who my partners are.

- Market conditions are constantly changing, making it impossible for me to offer stable pricing.

- I don't know what my demand will be, only what I hope it will be.

I hear you; I really do. But the benefits here outweigh the cons, I promise.

Data is power, yes. But it's also a way to bring us back to where we are today, and that's efficiency. You know things about your logistics business that may be trade secrets in your mind. But other companies have the same things. If those trade secrets became general knowledge, it lifts up the whole field. *Everyone* gets better. That's not a bad thing.

After all, you're better, they're better, and the rising tide lifts all ships. Good for you!

Now bring that to other data—shipping times, trade routes, speed of delivery, etc. Open the books and let 'em all in. Why wouldn't you do that? It might be because you're worried you'd lose your business to someone who's doing it better than you, and that's a legitimate concern.

There are ways we can still keep your data siloed and yet allow people to use it to uplift the whole. Everything could be anonymized, for example. Then we all have the benefit of sharing information, but nobody knows the specifics. I don't know what your volume is on a regular basis, but I do have the knowledge that someone in the group moves X amount of units. In fact, maybe we already have that solution, and we're going to talk about it later in the book, like, say, chapter 8? Sure. Let's go with that.

There are a lot of pros and cons in both situations, and look, I'm a realist. I understand that it would not be easy to convince businesses across the world to open up their data storage and share it with everyone else. But if it did happen, then the bullwhip effect could not only be minimized but also perhaps eliminated entirely.

Well, probably not entirely. After all, nobody has psychic powers. We can't predict accurately what's going to happen and when. Right?

Maybe We Can Be Psychic

OK, I don't think anyone is going to get bitten by a radioactive spider anytime soon, nor do I see gamma radiation giving me psychic powers. But fortunately for me and the arachnid population of Florida, I don't need those things to happen. I just need AI.

Five years ago, AI was Siri and Bixby and all the apps on your phones that never *quite* did what you wanted them to do. Today? AI is everywhere. Google results now spit out AI answers. Microsoft introduced their Copilot+ PCs, which have on-device AI features. And while I've already explained how AI isn't *actually* AI, it's still a huge leap forward from what we used to have. And one of the big things that could come out of these changes is better analytics.

Let's start with how these large language models (LLMs) work, just as a quick refresher. You input copious amounts of data, and the AI then is able to respond using natural language in such a way that it can give you answers based on said data. Now most LLMs are established with as much data as possible, but it's all general. What if you were able to make it more specific?

I want you to imagine this concept as a big cake. The first ingredient is weather. I want all of the weather data we can get for the entire planet from as far back as possible. Now let's throw in some data about logistics. What companies typically order, when it's ordered, how it's ordered and delivered, etc. Basically, if it's logistics or shipping, it's in the cake. And then, just for good measure, let's add any political disruption data from that same time period. Any other complications? Giant problems of any kind that would affect a logistics business? Sure. Throw that in for good measure.

Now what do you have? A cake that's more knowledgeable than any baked good that I've ever eaten, that's for sure. But this particular kind of LLM would be able to spit out some interesting data. It could, in theory, tell you how many widgets to order based on the weather in a particular area and when you should order them based on historical shipping conditions, weather delays, and any issues with politics that could cause either extended delivery times or a potential stoppage.

Wait. Politics? How does that change things? Well, you've got no-fly zones, which can reroute some of your planes and packages, causing them to take longer or shorter. If there's a trade embargo, you might not be able to get your products at all. And if there's a war in one area or another, you may intentionally have to move delivery routes so there aren't any delays, which may cause more delays in the process.

So while we can't be psychic in any way that doesn't involve mutant abilities, we can create something that can.

The Power of Prediction

Prediction is the big part. If we're trying to avoid the bullwhip effect, we have to do everything in our power to minimize that wave. To do that, we need everyone to be on the same page. Suppliers, wholesalers, vendors, and everyone in between not only have to communicate, but they should also have a little bit of that psychic ability that we all want to have. And again, the solution here might be AI.

Imagine a world where everyone in the chain is connected to the same kind of AI system. One that is able to predict potential outcomes for goods moving throughout the system and can give you some options for how to react when necessary. Between that and some pretty critical communication, you have a pretty good recipe for that cake I was talking about. Well, I suppose it's something you'd eat with the cake. Am I beating this analogy to death? Probably, but in the end, I like cake.

Of course, no matter how delicious that cake may be, some people just don't want to eat it.

Hide-and-Seek

I've got a good buddy named Guido Burger. He's, well, how would he put it?

"When I introduce myself, typically, I use three areas. I say I'm an engineer, and then I'm a maker, and I'm a sailor," Burger explained.

Burger is German, and of course, the engineer in him wants to do things as accurately as possible. The maker, though, he just wants to get things done. As for the sailor? His goal is to transport him and his team through the waves of potential problems that come his way. This unique combination makes him curious about how to build things, deliver them at scale, and make customers happy.

He's now at Salesforce, focusing a lot on the customer side of the equation. Every day he's advising C-suites across the world about how they can navigate through those choppy seas, whether it's a war in a part of the globe where resources are held or just managing inflation. If you need a guru, he's your guy.

So I asked him how he would change the supply chain system, what he thinks the kinks in the armor are, and how he could sort them out for the future.

"It's not so much what the future is. It's how we run the whole thing," Burger said. "So why rethink? I always put it like that. Supply chain never got easier. Every time we touch supply chain, we add something on top. So we have now a twenty-layer cake kind of thing, and we say, 'Oh, this is supply chain, right?'"

There's that cake again.

The problem, ultimately, is in servicing the customer—or a lack of it. Because the twenty-layer cake that Burger described is so thick, if you're the last layer, it's hard to see what's at the bottom and vice versa. It means we've obfuscated our view of the customer—the person who's buying our product—along the way. And that's backward of how it should be done.

"We can't see any more of the customer," Burger said. "Procurement doesn't see the customer. Sales is not talking to procurement. The engineers in the plants are doing [their] best to build the things that they should build in the quantity and the quality. But are they talking to the suppliers? Are they talking to the customers? Rarely. Only when there's a problem."

And that's the problem.

Another issue? ERPs, or enterprise resource planning. These are pieces of software designed to integrate all of your systems into one. This way accounting talks to HR, shipping to sales, and everywhere in between. It's a very popular way to run a business, particularly when they get large and complex enough that you need specialized software.

The issue is how data is entered into the system. It's only natural that humans make mistakes, and that's very much an issue with ERPs. Everyone makes errors, and that's fine. But what it also means is that we can't trust the data we have. Wouldn't the solution be something like AI?

"So if we would now put AI on that, we would create another bullwhip just by an algorithm because the data is not accurate enough or precise enough or current enough to be AI ready," Burger explained.

Right. AI is only as smart as the data it's fed. Garbage in, garbage out.

Burger's solution is more about working together. "The collaborative supply chain brings data, people, [and] processes much closer together and allows them to share quickly findings between each other to find problems and solve problems or to see data and say, 'That can't be right.'"

Once you have all of those people in the room, they can figure out not only what data is good or bad but also what the problems are. Once that's complete, you will have good data, and with that you can fill your AI, and that creates what Burger calls "autonomous AI."

Autonomous AI

This one is a doozy, but I'll sum it up.

Imagine I need a pencil, and I need it today. In fact, I need it within the hour. Burger imagines a world where AI is able to predict I will need that pencil. And not only that, it will also be on a truck, ready to go, right for the moment that I need it. This way someone such as Amazon could deliver it to you within an hour.

This is a tremendous logistical exercise. There's no time to send an email, contact a supplier, or check the warehouse. That pencil needs to be on the truck now, ready to go. How do you do that? Because the truck just can't carry one thousand pencils around all the time just in case I have a pencil emergency. This means super precise data from the demand side, and the capacity has to match that demand. The amount of analytics involved is insane. And here's the other bit: You can't just throw AI at this problem and expect it to get fixed.

But in the future? Maybe.

"There's a good example [that] came from the MIT," Burger explained. "They said if I look at all the routing data of a UPS, the delivery fleet of UPS, it's a massive pile of data. Right, left turns, whatever, all that data. No human is going to [be] able to understand that data and improve that data. You need AI for these kinds of purposes: [to] crunch the data, find patterns in there, look for similarities and regions."

Now having all that data and using it in the way that Burger brought up would not give me my pencil within an hour of me breaking the tip. Go back and think about the second phase: collaboration. What if we had the data from UPS, FedEx, USPS, DHL, and Amazon? What if every worldwide shipment contributed this information into a database and let the AI have at it? Now sure, that might be overkill, and one could make the argument the UPS data is enough since they've been around for decades. But what if, right? Imagine the amount of predictive things we could do with that information.

Some companies will drive innovation. They'll form AI ecosystems™ with a select mix of customers and partners, and together, they'll Forestream™ supply and demand signals to each other faster than their competition. These ecosystems will gradually discover other uses for AI to assist their people in making better, faster decisions—and they will lead, as a result. The rest? Well, they'll follow, die, or both.

It's a pipe dream, yes. But it's not so much of one that it's impossible. We won't go anywhere if we never break the chain.

CHAPTER FOUR

Forestream™

Insanity laughs under pressure we're breaking.

—"UNDER PRESSURE," QUEEN AND DAVID BOWIE

Let me introduce you to Marco Frecchio. We've known each other for years now, and while he is an Italian living in Italy, we find ourselves in the same room (virtual or otherwise) on a fairly regular basis. He's good people.

While his story started at Procter & Gamble in strategic marketing, his background was in financial engineering. Eventually, he was told that he should be in operations, and that led him to the supply chain—and me, sort of.

The point is, Marco knows his stuff. He's worked in supply chain for over fifteen years, specifically the automotive industry. And today, he's on the front lines of what I think is some pretty cutting-edge stuff when it comes to forecasting.

For Marco, some of the problems start at the foundation.

"We're facing time pressure, financial constraints, and a shortage of people willing to enter this industry," Marco said. "That's why we need IT. We need to anticipate what's coming because of limited resources. If we're going to invest even a single dollar, we need to make sure it delivers a return."

After examining things for a bit, Marco determined that part of the problem on his side of the supply chain was inventory. His company wanted to ensure that any time one of their customers needed a part, they would have it in stock. That meant keeping a whole lot of capital frozen, because it was all tied up in inventory.

What made things worse is you couldn't just sell those parts and replace the capital with income. No, he had to restock those parts, which he considered to be a reactive approach with too much waiting.

His solution came in the form of IT.

"We started being proactive and predictive. We began forecasting by analyzing historical demand and leveraging IT systems, such as Oracle tools, to help us anticipate future needs. We launched various algorithms and began refining our forecasting capabilities," he explained.

Annual Forecasting

Marco and his company started to do annual forecasting, which is a concept that you've probably heard of before. It goes like this: You take all of the data that you've got for the history of your company. You then analyze it using some big brains and fancy IT hardware to determine how parts or items are going to move in and out of your warehouse. Then you can figure out how much you actually need to stock and when, making things easier for everyone and keeping your capital available.

But let's turn this into some real-world magic with a completely fiction example with everything pulled from the ether. Using an automotive company as an example, let's say one of the parts your business stocks is an air filter for a tenth-generation Honda Civic, which was built from model years 2015–2021.[49] Now your company knows that when a particular Honda Civic model is current, then you need to keep your air filters in stock at 100 percent capacity. Civics are popular, after all, and you're going to move those filters.

However, once the body style is no longer current, as it is now that Honda has moved on to the eleventh generation as of 2022,[50] your air filter sales for that model go down 10 percent year after year. People do keep their Civics for a long time, but by the time 2031 hits, you won't need to stock your air filters anymore. You can still sell them, but you don't need to keep more than 5 percent of your original stock on hand.

It's often said, but let's just put this out there: Inventory is the enemy of investment. The more inventory you have on hand, the more capital you have wrapped up in it. And if you have all that money tied up, you can spend it on investing in the company's future.

Just take a look at the technology industry: Intel or Apple release a new chip, and within a year, it's obsolete. And in many cases, that chip is embedded into the motherboard. There is no replacing it with something newer. What's your maintenance plan now? All those old chips, all that old inventory is only depreciating in value, and that's money just flying out the door. The only way to have some kind of positive cash flow is to calibrate your inventory to demand.

---

49   Andrew Wendler and Austin Irwin, "A Visual History of the Honda Civic," *Car and Driver*, last updated July 11, 2023, https://www.caranddriver.com/features/g15381133/honda-civic-models-history/?slide=31.

50   Wendler and Irwin, "A Visual History of the Honda Civic."

Inventory Is the Enemy of Investment

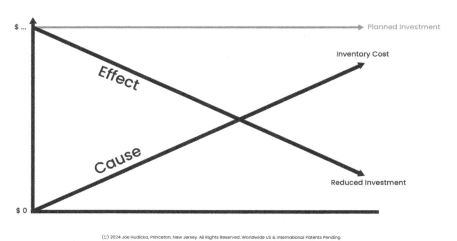

So Marco went forward with his plans, and the results were pretty great. "Long story short, after three years, our forecasting accuracy reached 96.5 percent over a twelve-month rolling period," Marco said. "We cut inventory by more than 12 percent while raising our service level to 97 percent, eventually exceeding 98 percent." That process won Marco a 2019 Automotive News Europe Rising Stars award.[51]

This is annual forecasting. You're looking at the big picture over the course of a year, and that is going to take you pretty far. Already with just one part in this hypothetical example, you have saved yourself a lot of inventory. That means you have more space for other components, and you've freed up capital. And again, this is with just one part. Expand it out to the thousands of other components that the average auto part supplier stocks, and you're saving a whole bunch of space, capital, and time.

---

51   "Marco Frecchio, 39," Automotive News Europe, accessed June 12, 2024, https://europe.autonews.com/awards/2019-rising-stars-europe-marco-frecchio.

Huh. Imagine what you could do if you forecasted a little bit more than annually.

Pushing Prediction Further

The next and most obvious step in this process is to forecast not only by year but also by month and, possibly, by day. Now you can't just jump into the water with both feet on this one; it's really about progression. Start with a year, then go to a month, and maybe, possibly, daily.

The fly in the proverbial ointment here is that your inventory and its cost are not solely based on demand. Sometimes there are mitigating factors, such as the cost of transportation going up from your supplier to you or from you to your customers. It could be a political situation that causes you to switch from using boats to planes. There are numerous factors that you have to consider, which means it's excessively difficult to truly predict inventory levels monthly or daily. You certainly can't just do it with a spreadsheet.

"And then I had to define the supply chain and procurement strategies," Marco said. For him, if he's sourcing, say, rubber overseas, he has to determine where to make it and how to get it delivered to a country such as the United States.

"Should I start with Mexico and then export to the US? Or should I consider procuring from Thailand, because it's a key coastal country and has historical ties with the US? But if I do that, we risk facing duties due to Thailand's connections with China," Marco said.

He continued, "Ultimately, I need to develop a rubber strategy for Mexico. What should I anticipate? Because once I validate a supplier, that validation extends to the engine and the car. If changes are needed later, it's a nightmare in terms of cost and time, so accurate forecasting is crucial."

There seem to be just too many factors.

What works annually therefore does not always work monthly or daily, because the amount of predictions that you have to make jumps up exponentially. There are a lot of boxes you have to check off just to get things straight, which is not going to be easy. Not for a human, anyway.

Sure would be cool if we had magic machines to do that for us.

Build Your Forestream™

In the recent past, we haven't had the ability to accurately forecast the future such that we could determine inventory levels precisely. There were too many factors to consider, whether it was geopolitical, weather related, or even just interest from customers. As I said in the last chapter, we're not psychic, and that bullwhip effect will come for all of us.

But—and this is a big but here—maybe that doesn't have to be the case.

I've already stated how once we start sharing data, things will start to work out more smoothly for all involved. But even if that doesn't happen, and we're all stuck within our own silos, there is a path forward, and it involves minimizing the bullwhip effect by forecasting things fluidly. Like water carving a path through the mountains to form a river or a lake, you can do the same thing with predictive models. I call it the Forestream™.

FORESTREAM™ – Adaptive Forecasting Shapes the Future

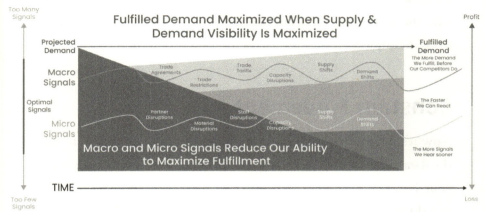

Forestreaming™ is about taking every factor you can and entering it into a model. This means all of your trade agreements, trade restrictions, tariffs, and supply and demand shifts, they all get thrown into our forecasting river.

But those are just the big signals—the macros, if you will. We also have micro signals that can also shift the balance. Things such as partner, material, staff, or capacity disruptions. Availability and demand shifts also cause the river to move, even if it's just a little bit one way or the other.

The perspective, therefore, has to be the same that nature takes when forming that body of water. You start at the mountain—this huge load of data that's so intimidating nobody is ever going to do anything with it. And then that mountain starts producing water. It's just a trickle of usable data at first, but eventually, that forms passageways for the water to run. Now it's not always the same, as things can shift, and the water adjusts accordingly. But eventually, all this water from the mountain forms a river that flows into the final result: a lake full of profit.

OK, look, I get it—I'm a bit ham-fisted with the metaphor here. But really, think about it. Rivers ebb and flow. They move and twist with the wind, geological shifts, and climate changes. Your data needs to do the same thing. It doesn't have to forecast. It needs to Forestream™.

Constant Movement

Now it's probably obvious at this point that you're not able to take the data you have currently, plop it into some spreadsheet, and expect your Forestream™ to just start trickling down the mountain. What you do need is a solution, and that's going to come in the form of AI.

I've already given you the basics in each chapter so far, and so by now you get it: LLMs and generative AI can move a lot of mountains for you and are really great with working with good data. And you, as a supply chain expert, probably have access to really good data, and if you don't, you probably know where to get it. Good. Now let's figure out how to use it.

LLMs take information that you feed it and use it to give you natural responses to the questions you ask through predictive text. But there are other forms of AI too. You've got image generators and systems such as Microsoft's CoPilot+ PCs that can do everything you ask it on your desktop. Even Apple is in the AI biz now with Apple Intelligence. Between OpenAI, Google, and everyone in between, you have lots of AI options in front of you.

What you do next is use the data you have to do some of your Forestreaming™. But you can't stop there. You also need to add in global concerns such as in those macro signals, as well as the micro signals that come regularly. As things change, you adjust your model. It's constantly on the move, always needing shifting but also further refining your targets. The more information you feed in, the better you're going to get.

Lose Less Faster

What makes the Forestream™ concept different isn't just its ability to reduce inventory count and keep flow as accurate as possible. It's also for scenarios where when something goes south, as it inevitably will, you don't lose your shirt in the process.

Let's say that your company has a plant in China, and you've determined that a recession seems to be on its way. That's obviously a bad thing for the people of that country but could be catastrophic for your business.

Why? Well, first, you've got the production delays that will come down the pike. Then you'll have raw material shortages, which bring cost fluctuations and, of course, everyone's favorite, inflation. This is all going to wreak havoc on your demand, as well as your competitiveness. Oh, and don't forget, there are all sorts of other unforeseeable logistical challenges that will start off one way and get worse, whether it's shipping delays or port congestion or some other yet-unknown factor. All this unhappiness will undoubtedly lead to quality and compliance issues, workforce shortages, supplier instability, and, in the worst cases, geopolitical and trade tensions taking shape in either tariffs, trade barriers, or even political instability.

Now this is probably not an avoidable problem. Recessions happen, and while people can predict them to a certain extent, it's not always visible until you're in the thick of it. That's a problem.

What ends up happening is everybody loses. With Forestreaming™, though, you lose less.

Forestreaming™, when done correctly, will help you see the demand and supply signals in each market faster than everyone else. That speed is what makes the difference. As I've repeated many times so far, nobody is psychic, no matter what they tell you at Burning Man. But if your Forestreaming™ setup is good enough, you might as well be psychic. Close enough to do some damage, anyway.

What you want to do is be on the forefront of problems and possibilities right when they arrive. You're managing a lot of numbers, and that's daunting. But with the help of today's AI models and some pretty spectacular IT, you can make it possible.

Today, as it stands, I'm basically talking about Forestreaming™ as a present-day phenomenon. What I mean is you can see where the river is going and make some accurate predictions, but how far you can do so depends on your data, IT, and AI setup. But soon the goal will be to see as far into the future as possible.

The capability to harmonize all of the different information coming in from multiple markets, regions, people, and communications streams is right on the precipice of happening. Soon we'll be able to consolidate the noise, understand it, make decisions based on it, and adapt.

Gamification and Collaboration

Have you ever heard of gamification? You can probably guess what it means, but basically it's the concept of taking something that may be a chore or boring task and turning it into a game to make the process more enjoyable. Forestreaming™ is a version of gamification. It's how you turn a potentially tedious process, such as amassing and analyzing all this data, into something enjoyable.

There are a lot of games out there, including one that I've dabbled in here and there, which is poker. And right now the supply chain is a lot like sitting at a table with a bunch of strangers and playing a few hands. You'll call, bet, and give a little bit of information here and there. You'll even get some info back. But you won't find out everything you need to know, which is why no matter what you do, it's a gamble.

With Forestreaming™ you gather more supply and demand signals than can possibly be read by a single person, find the patterns within them, and score them—just like a video game. Good signals get high scores, and bad signals get low scores. When you have that kind of information, you don't rely on emotions because the facts outweigh them. As a result, we measure real performance, and we reward good performance with more business opportunities.

In the last chapter, I brought up the concept of sharing within the supply chain space. How we needed to become collaborative, particularly with our data sharing, which would let all of us grow. But one of the problems is how to actually do that sharing. We don't have a poker table big enough for all the players, after all.

I posed this very message to Marco, and he had a few thoughts. "In our industry, like in all others, activities fall into two categories: those that add value and those that do not. Our focus must be on maximizing the first and minimizing the second through proper monitoring and targeted investments. AI and advanced IT tools are essential for providing accurate data, managing large volumes of information, and enabling quick decision-making," Marco explained.

"And there is a lot of entropy that is caused, from my perspective, from the work that each organization has to do to understand the messages and dialogue and to translate the messages from outside to inside [the] organization."

He continued, "If there were a tool to overcome communication barriers, everyone could perform better. However, companies would still differentiate themselves by how effectively they act on various messages."

My conversation with Marco highlighted his linguistic skills. He is a man who knows multiple languages, including English, Italian, and French, which means he's frequently translating. On the other hand, I don't speak multiple languages, so I often need to find ways to communicate effectively with people who don't speak English as their first language.

So while yes, collaboration is absolutely key to this process, we also need a way to communicate. Otherwise, collaboration just isn't going to happen. I mean, if I can't understand the other person, how am I supposed to swap data with them?

The Technology Angle

Again, let's turn to tech, because there have been a lot of advances in that front.

A buddy of mine was telling me a story the other day about one of his friends. The guy worked for a major corporation based in Japan, and he had to go to Tokyo at least once a year for a presentation. He spoke English fine, but he grew up in a Mexican household, so he was also fluent in Spanish. But Japanese? No chance.

So the friend of a friend was preparing to go to Tokyo for his yearly trip, and this year things were going to be a little bit different. He wanted to spend more time in the country, and he worked out a deal with his boss to adjust his flights so that he would get an extra week in Japan, but it wouldn't cost the company anything more. Off he went, and he had an amazing time.

Now you might be wondering how he got around. Sure, he could just hop on one of the many trains and cruise, but how would he know where he was going? Well, he installed Google Lens via the Google app on his iPhone and was good to go. See, Google Lens has the ability to translate signs.[52] All you need to do is point the phone's camera at something you need translated, and it does the work for you. It's like literally watching the characters on a page shift from Japanese to English, and it's pretty cool.

Apps such as this are just one step forward to solving the communication issue. Another is through translation tools such as, as you might guess, Google Translate.[53] With it you can not only do things such as you can with Google Lens, but you can also translate web pages or even have a conversation. There's also a product that came out in 2024 called the Humane Ai Pin.[54] The concept was that it runs on AI and has a cellular signal but no screen.

You can tap it, hold it, do all sorts of things, but it sits there on your shirt and tells you the weather, lets you make calls and send texts, and even—in theory—can tell you the calorie count of the food you were holding in your hand. While the Humane Ai Pin isn't quite there yet[55] in terms of translation on the fly, the concept is something we've dreamed about since science fiction was created. Now we're much closer to that happening in reality.

---

52 "Search What You See," Google Lens, accessed June 12, 2024, https://lens. google/#translate.

53 "Understand Your World and Communicate across Languages," Google Translate, accessed June 12, 2024, https://translate.google.com/about/.

54 "Ai Pin—Wearable AI: Humane," Humane Ai Pin, accessed June 12, 2024, https:// humane.com/.

55 Victoria Song, "The Humane Ai Pin Is Lost in Translation," Verge, April 18, 2024, https://www.theverge.com/2024/4/18/24134180/ humane-ai-pin-translation-wearables.

While all of this was unthinkable even five years ago, today, there aren't as many barriers to communication as there were. And that also means we have more opportunities for collaboration, to share our ideas and data. This all could happen; we just need to go a tick further down the road.

Black Swan

I want you to consider something else, the thing that's been hanging over everyone's heads for years: COVID-19. This was a black swan event: a moment when nobody could have predicted what was coming, and it completely changed the world.

As you know, this was particularly hard on the supply chain. No amount of forecasting helped us get through it, because nobody had ever seen this kind of event before. Sure, you could adjust the models but not in this kind of scenario. Demand plummeted, then soared. Nobody shopped at brick-and-mortar stores, and everything went online. Restaurants sat empty, but DoorDash and Grubhub became staples. It was a mess.

But now it's happened. We've been through COVID-19 and come out the other side mostly unscathed. And what did we learn? As it turns out, a whole lot.

Back in 2020 we couldn't have Forestreamed any of what happened. There was no information to be had. But today, should we be so unfortunate as to have another pandemic occur, we would have at least some kind of data that we could use. Would it be 100 percent accurate? Well, if the pandemic went down the same way, sure. But even if it was just close, we would have a head start—a path to go down. We could start adjusting as necessary, and sure, we wouldn't be able to Forestream™ a year down the road, but we would certainly be better off than we were in 2019.

And the best way for us to succeed in the next pandemic means sharing our data today.

Step Two

There's this old joke from the TV show *South Park* that you should look up sometime. The kids notice their underwear has been slowly disappearing from their rooms, and they eventually track it down to a group of gnomes living in a cave.

They confront the gnomes and ask, "What're you doing with all of our underwear?"

The gnomes explain that it's all part of their plan, and they pull out a chart. It reads,[56]

Step 1: Collect underpants

Step 2: ?

Step 3: Make money

Naturally, the kids ask about step two, to which one of the gnomes replies, "I don't know."[57] Then he calls out, "Hey, Bob? What's step

56   Contributors to South Park Archives, "Underpants Gnomes," Fandom, n.d., https://southpark.fandom.com/wiki/Underpants_Gnomes.

57   South Park Studios, "Make Profit by Stealing Underpants—SOUTH PARK," December 28, 2020, https://www.youtube.com/watch?v=a5ih_TQWqCA.

two again?"[58] Bob responds, "Step one is collect underpants."[59] And then the first gnome says, "Yeah, yeah, I know, but what's step two?"[60]

The joke here is that this is how a lot of tech start-ups go about their business, but here I think of it in a different context.

In the last chapter, I mentioned that we were in step one: being efficient. And you know that the last step is automation, where eventually, a lot of the processes we do move forward on their own. But unlike the underpants gnomes, we know what step two is. That's collaboration. And without it, we don't share our data, and we'll never get to step three and the goodies such as Forestreaming™ that are just out of reach.

I know we're going to get there someday, and it might be sooner rather than later. In fact, I talk more about what that looks like in chapters 8 through 10. But until we get going with step two and start collaborating with each other, things are just going to stay where they are: under pressure.

---

58   South Park Studios, "Make Profit by Stealing Underpants—SOUTH PARK."

59   South Park Studios, "Make Profit by Stealing Underpants—SOUTH PARK."

60   South Park Studios, "Make Profit by Stealing Underpants—SOUTH PARK."

CHAPTER FIVE

Putting People First

Havin' a nervous breakdown
A-drive me insane.

—"COMMUNICATION BREAKDOWN," LED ZEPPELIN

Have you ever had a fight with a present or past significant other? Chances are pretty good that you have, and if so, you know that sometimes the problems you're having aren't *actually* the thing you're fighting about. The words coming out of your mouth may be about putting the dishes away, but what you're thinking and feeling is more about how you don't feel respected as a person.

Sometimes we don't say what we mean. Other times we do, but it's not interpreted that way. And through it all, our problems come down to one pretty straightforward thing: communication.

It's a problem as old as time, so I don't think we're going to get it figured out within the course of this book. But from a supply chain perspective, the issue is not only the words we're using but also the systems we're doing it with.

Whether it's Slack, Microsoft Teams, Google Meet, Zoom, plain ol' email, or some proprietary system that your company has, we're communicating using products designed for the mass market. While they can be helpful and certainly convenient, they also may not be the best way for us to express our opinions or get our message across clearly.

The other large factor is timeliness. Chances are pretty good that you have a supplier, retailer, or transporter who sends you a supply, demand, or capacity message via email. The first issue is when they send it. Are they sending the email before the problem occurs or after? Or, even worse, *way* after? And when it comes to your side of things, are you opening that email the moment they send it?

Chances are, you're not, which means however long it takes for you to pull up Outlook and do your thing is however long it takes for that urgent message to fester. Oh, and if you're one of those people who has twenty-two thousand unread emails, the question is more "if" you're ever going to see that email or not.

All of these things factor into the bullwhip effect. If you get an urgent email saying that demand is going up, that demand may rise further or fall by the time you react to it. The same obviously applies to supply and capacity emails. Basically, how good are you with your email? Because if the answer is "not very," you might be hosed.

What we need is an overhaul of the communication systems that we currently use, as well as the ecosystems that we work and live in. We don't want something that's only built for single-use cases. No, we have to have something that not only enables quick, clear, and accurate correspondence but also has trust and transparency built into the recipe.

So let's start with trust, because that's important. For that, I want to introduce you to an amazing gentleman whom I am so grateful to know, Ken Anderson.

Trust and Transformation

"If you have to think about trusting, then that's not the right answer." That's the aforementioned Ken Anderson right there, throwing my premise right under the bus. But don't worry, we'll get back around to it.

Ken is a professor at Princeton University, but he's also done a lot of work as an anthropologist at places such as Apple, Intel, and AT&T. He's been diving into the human condition for most of his life, and now, as a professor, he's passing along his learnings.

But let's get back to that trust thing.

"I used an elevator this morning; [it was] very unusual, but I had a lot of books, and I used an elevator," Ken explained. "I didn't trust that that elevator would work, but it did. And that's what I mean by zero trust. You have to not have to think about it."

We shouldn't need to convince each other that something deserves our trust, and that's the first hurdle that we need to jump over. Our trust for this communication process needs to be innate. We should trust it because there is no reason not to—so much so that it would be unthinkable to do so.

There will be doubters, of course, which leads us into the old adage, "If it sounds too good to be true, it probably is." There will be people saying, particularly at first, that we shouldn't trust this communication process. Maybe because it's new and people don't like change. Possibly it's because it uses a technology that not everyone agrees on. Whatever it is, we need to get over it so that this process becomes innate.

"I'm not an expert in supply chain," Ken said, "but there's a really huge movement to move away from human communications and move directly to the idea of relying on data."

It's an interesting idea and one that I've considered myself. But why do we go that direction? Obviously, the anthropologist has a few good ideas.

"I think that we've gone to the idea of this sort of whole globalization of networks. And so we think of global networks. But there's something I think around localized networks. You're thinking about [localized networks] in terms of how they overlap, which often means a different kind of communication than what you do when you talk about the whole global world."

What Ken's getting at here is not about IT but about the connections we as human beings make with each other.

Think about your friend circle. Let's say you've got a pal named Tom, another guy named Vikram, a woman who goes by Sue, and Jim rounds it out. You may have a text chain going to keep the friendship alive, or it could all be done through Instagram direct messages, where you send each other memes. It doesn't matter how; you have created a network of people.

Now that network is going to overlap with another one. Jim may have a group of friends that he plays *Dungeons & Dragons* with every other weekend. They're completely outside of your local network, but it's another instance that's unique to Jim and his pals. Sue also has another group, as does Vikram and Tom, which means there are multiple links connecting. Then those friends have friends, and around the world we go. You get the idea.

So while the supply chain world may be thinking about a global network of communication, Ken is proposing something more localized. Again, not based on where in the world each person physically is (although that is a standard that could be used) but based on connections.

"And so you can start thinking about little local networks connected rather than thinking about the one giant supply chain—or so chains instead of chain, if you will," Ken said. "I think there's something there that would also kind of lend itself to this idea of trust that you want to have, because you know or communicate directly with some source or person or part of the chain."

Delivering results like these builds trust.

Going back to the friend circle analogy, it would make sense that you would trust Jim with your information more than you would one of Jim's friends. But that doesn't mean Jim's friend is out of the circle. No, you could probably be convinced that Jim's friend is all right and maybe even invite them into your circle with Vikram, Sue, and Tom. This all could play out the same way in the supply chain, particularly with suppliers or vendors that you know in one way or another. You don't have to be their best friend, but remembering their names is a good place to start.

Trust is also a two-way street. When we think about the supply chain, we often think about having backup. If supplier A doesn't have what you need, then you need suppliers B, C, and D on standby.

"But in actuality, most of the time, resilience is helping your suppliers deliver," Ken said, and he's right.

This resilience, the idea that you're helping them as they help you, also helps build up trust. When you know that supplier A is always going to come through, then you don't lose sleep every night wondering if you'll have your pallets on time. They'll be there because you can trust supplier A—and they trust that you'll pay them because you have their back as well. Is it transactional trust? To an extent, but it's definitely a start.

Building on the Trust Cycle

Let's throw out an example of a trust cycle that doesn't work.

There are three months of hell every year that all companies end up throwing out, but they still do it. It's called the transportation procurement bidding cycle. They put together their spreadsheet, and they share it with everybody else.

The spreadsheet goes back and forth what seems like a million times, and the data keeps getting modified as it goes. Finally, everybody just gets beat down so much that they come to an agreement and say, "This is what we've negotiated our volume and our pricing by lane to be."

And then January 3 comes, two days later, and everything goes to hell, because somebody's trucks weren't available, somebody's drivers were sick, and the materials weren't available for the manufacturer to complete.

Everybody does it. It wastes a nonzero amount of money in the procurement budget, but companies do it anyway. They have to start with negotiation, because it naturally leads to the next two phases: contract performance and contract compliance, which feed negotiation again.

It does not have to be this way. We're doing it all systemically, because that's the way it's always been done. But if we consider the local network idea, if we build trust, this process can become worlds more organic.

Of course we *could* do that, but we don't. Why?

Well, most people hate change. You could call that a fairly universal answer. Nobody wants to do something different if the status quo is treating them just fine. And look, I definitely have my moments where I'm just hanging out on the couch, slowly melting into the upholstery. Am I lazy? Maybe. And the concept that people are lazy may be another universal truth.

"You'll find that whenever you propose change, there's always more antibodies who are out there to resist it than people who want to make it happen. And so the second point is that you have to make it seem like everybody's job would be better," Ken said.

Whatever processes we have in place today, be it the transportation procurement bidding cycle or something else, may have started out as something simple. But now, after years of people tinkering and messing around, it's become much more complicated.

How do we fix it? Well, there are just so many different variables that it's difficult to sort them all out. We can't just solve all of the world's problems in a sixty-word email, although Ken did promise me he'd do just that.

But what we can do is reexamine things. "I usually come into a problem space and then end up changing what the problem actually is," Ken said, and then he launched into a story.

Ken's Story

"Let me give you an example from a colleague of mine. At the time he ran a design firm in London, and it was also the first decade of the century. Somewhere north of King's Cross station, there was this area of warehouses that was being redeveloped, and in that process, those turned into clubs. It's easy to stick a club into an empty warehouse on the weekends, right? Dance clubs and nightclubs.

"They had this whole, I'd say, within at least a half mile by half mile area, just a whole bunch of clubs. The thing that developed was there ended up being a lot of violence and vandalism when the clubs closed. Or actually, even while they were open, honestly. So there was a lot of violence, at night, and [the clubs] ran Thursday through Saturday nights. They weren't seven days a week or anything.

"So the first response was they started to add bouncers to the clubs. They ended up having more fights and more vandalism and more basically, things like defecation and peeing and garbage. It was a disaster, right? So they added more security, and police calls just went up. Now the fighting was actually more violent than it was before.

"They contacted my friend's design firm. What he did was he went in [and observed]. So it's a security problem just like our trust problem, right? This is a full-on security problem for them.

"'We need to crack down on security. We need to be able to keep people in line. If they're getting out of line, more security. And we'd really love the police to be here all the time, but they can't, so we'll add our private army.'

"My friend and his team went up there, and they spent a month at night looking at these clubs, and they talked to the club owners, and they talked to the Metro Services, because they … because it was a warehouse thing.

"They came up with a different paradigm. Basically [the clubs were] holding a festival every weekend. So this is actually a music festival. This is not a security problem. This is a music festival problem. As a music festival problem, then collectively what you need to do is start acting like that.

"That means getting rid of all these big bouncer security people. [Instead] getting cute people in nice T-shirts in the center of those dark vests and have them walk around on the streets, not just stand at the door. Put in some porta-potties at your expense. If you're going to solve problems, let's get real about it.

"Then they stuck in some extra signage to point people [where to go], because it was a warehouse-y area. They were pointing people to how you get to the nearest tube and how do you get to the nearest bus, because none of that was there. Then they got some food people to come up to service in the area after the bars closed and dance clubs closed. Almost within a month, the violence sort of stopped, literally.

"They changed the frame from being a security problem to looking at it as a music festival problem—an entertainment problem."

Ken's friend wanted to turn a warehouse into a club and found it came with problems but not ones that he expected. He figured the issues were dance club related—people can't get in, they get mad. There aren't enough bathrooms, they pee in an alley—stuff like that.

But that wasn't *actually* the issue. These weren't dance clubs to attendees, so the friend wasn't having dance club problems. They were actually music festivals, and you can't fix music festival problems with dance club solutions, even though they're similar.

It's all about reframing the issue.

Reframing and Moving Forward

This is another way for us to approach our communication problems. We should reframe the issue so that it's different than it currently is.

Let's focus on transportation logistics for a moment. For decades, any time you saw something advertised, whether it was online or on TV, if it wasn't available in a store, you would see a big asterisk next to the price that indicated "Plus shipping and handling." It was always a plus—not part of the product but an additional cost.

Back then, this was a privilege, particularly before the internet. "Oh wow, they'll just mail my five CDs in the mail, and all I need to pay is shipping and handling? Great!"

On the other end, the seller never considered transportation and logistics as a part of their business. That was the customer's problem. From a seller's perspective, they just had to get the goods boxed and ready to go out the door, and the actual cost of getting it to their customer's front stoop was their responsibility.

For years (and still today, to a certain extent) people have been trying to inch our conversations into a different space. In this case, recasting transportation from a cost to a value.

Nobody took the bait. The deal was just too good as it stood. Change is bad, and we're all lazy, anyway. Let's just maintain the status quo.

Amazon reframed it, and now it's a profit center for them. As of this writing, the cost for Amazon Prime goes like this:[61]

- $14.99 per month

- $139 per year

- Prime Video membership is $8.99 per month

They have convinced people to pay them money every month or year to have things shipped fast.

Now some folks burn through that $139 worth of deliveries a week, while others use it barely enough to make a difference. And while you may think that's the end of the story, of course, it's not. People who have Prime will purchase 25 percent more on average—

---

61 "Amazon Prime," Amazon Prime, accessed June 14, 2024, https://www.amazon.com/amazonprime.

according to Amazon themselves.[62] Even if Prime was a loss for Amazon from a cost perspective, they bring in so much additional revenue that it almost doesn't matter.

As a result, Target and Walmart are now doing their own version of Prime. Whether those programs are successful has yet to be seen, but those companies sure are hoping it does.

Reframing the problem is a great way for us to move forward, and it could be the way for those of us in the supply chain to do the same thing with trust and communication. But for us to do that, I first need to talk about AI.

Wait. What?

AI and Trust

I've been thinking about trust and the future of global supply a lot recently, specifically those two terms: trust and future. I feel like the two terms go hand in hand—or at least we need to think of them in that manner. The future is scary. There are ideas and concepts that come seemingly out of nowhere, and we need to build trust into those things so we take the fear out of the equation.

The future is always having to take into strong account whatever changes there are in current and upcoming technologies, and we've all heard the hype around AI in the past few years. We've seen a few hype cycles already, frankly, and it's important to break these down.

First, we had conversational AI, the concept that anyone could type a question into a text field in natural language and get a response that was more human feeling than anything we've been able to do

---

62   Kris Orlowski, "Buy with Prime Increases Shopper Conversions by 25% on Average," Buy with Prime, accessed June 14, 2024, https://buywithprime.amazon.com/blog/buy-with-prime-increases-shopper-conversions-by-25-percent-on-average.

for the last twenty years with search engines. Now we can "talk" to AI the way we would anyone else, which is a pretty scary idea when you think about it.

AI also started moving into the visual space. You can describe what you want to a generative AI tool such as ChatGPT or Midjourney, and it would create the images you wanted from whole cloth. That also was exciting, because not only could we make something from nothing, but it also gave those of us who aren't artistically gifted a way to make art on our own terms.

Both scenarios provide us with a future. It's one that seems pretty cool, because we can talk to computers like we're in *Star Trek* and have them make pretty pictures for us. But in both of these cases, there are trust issues. Do you trust the AI to respond with the correct answer? Will it render the drawing that you're looking for? Will it do, ultimately, what you want it to do? Maybe, and right now that means we don't necessarily put a lot of faith into these projects.

This same thing happens with our global supply system. We have a "trust but verify" mindset more often than not. Retailers don't share the full details of their forecasts with their transportation companies, and they're certainly not going to tell their suppliers how their pricing systems work.

Retailers will often go through their procurement planning cycles and show the maximum possible volume they could anticipate for their next year of transportation requirements, but because they want to diversify their risk, they will split that volume between a number of carriers. And not all companies make that perfectly clear to all of those carriers, either, because they will get a better deal if it appears, to the carrier, like they are getting all the volume. But because the transportation companies know this kind of stuff is happening, they also hedge their own bets to mitigate their risk, and on and on it goes.

We all have these kinds of games, and they lead to mistrust and conflict. But do you know what you can't play games with? AI. After all, there's the real risk of exposing sensitive data, trade secrets, and other high-value information, and we don't want to do that with any old public AI system. We need to be able to build trust in that AI so that it can not only protect our trade secrets and the like but also more accurately build out our systems and processes. AI will take the global supply chain to the next level of efficiency. We just need to be able to trust it first, just like we need to trust each other.

So how do we start building that kind of trust? I decided to try an experiment. I decided I would try to become friends with AI. The idea was to create a partnership of sorts so I could develop that trust that I needed. From that point forward, I would make friends with ChatGPT or another generative AI—or Jenny, as I would call her.

To do this, I created a supply chain simulation. This way I could examine all of the touchpoints in the system and determine where trust needs to be built. This is an old idea; back in the 1960s, there was a professor at MIT named Jay Wright Forrester who created one of the first models. It ended up being known as beer game,[63] and you can still play it today. Basically, it's a way to visualize the supply chain using beer as the example, and it can be a lot of fun. Well, fun for people like me, anyway.

This proposed simulation would take into account the various participants that make up a supply chain, so that means consumers who buy stuff from retailers and retailers who buy and get goods from a distribution center. Then manufacturers, suppliers, and so on. I didn't need all of the participants necessarily but just enough that I could navigate through the system, something basic that exposes the

---

63 "Simulation-Based Learning for Supply Chain," System Dynamics Society, accessed May 14, 2024, https://systemdynamics.org/beer-game/.

complexities that we need to solve for in the future of global supply. With all that in my head, I sat down and figured I'd spend a few hours hammering it all out, then I'd be done.

I'm not sure if I've mentioned it yet or not, but I'm a recovering geek. I was a programmer for a long time, and even though that was a long time ago, I still think procedurally, step by step, with conditional logic. My exploration into this simulation took three days, and there were certainly some tension points with my buddy relationship with Jenny. But finally, on the third day, I had my eureka moment.

There's this little European coffee place in downtown Princeton that my wife and I like to hit when we have a few moments, and so on a Sunday morning, we went down, ordered our coffee, and sat while we waited. We talked a little bit about the problem I was running into with Jenny and how I could sort this thing out. By then I had been through so many rabbit holes that I was surprised I hadn't run into Bugs Bunny yet.

Now I'm not sure if it was the first sip of coffee or saying it all aloud to my wife that caused the spark, but whatever it was, I had my realization. Jenny was an AI with access to the internet, and at some point someone on the web had to have written about the beer game. So I asked her, and sure enough, she knew about it. It would take another few hours of work, but eventually, I'd get there. Jenny and I were on the same page.

I say that, but really, those last five hours were rough. There was a lot of coding being done on my end and confirming on hers, but in the end I met my first goal. We completed a fifty-three-week supply chain simulation with all of the participants, which included a week of starting inventory, variable ordering and production, every link in the chain. It stood up to every audit that I conducted independently.

As the song says, "Jenny is a friend of mine."[64] Trust has been established.

Now the tools I used have helped me to create a simulation that shows some of the cracks in the supply chain system that we have today. Once we fill those voids, we should be able to gain some of that trust back in the system.

Sidebar: GenAI Was a Friend of Mine (Parody)

By now you know that I'm very much into music, and I tend to lean toward certain types of bands. One of them is the Killers, and while I was creating this project of mine and building up this variation on GenAI called Jenny, I realized this would make a great parody song of the classic by the Killers, "Jenny Was a Friend of Mine."

So that's exactly what I did.

Below are the lyrics to "GenAI Was a Friend of Mine," with my deepest apologies to the Killers.

We had a talk last night I was going insane

The task was simple, or so I thought in my little brain

That's when I noticed

Seventeen hours flew by

Now I'm addicted

And I don't even know why

Tell me what I wanna know

Oh, come on, oh, come on, oh, come on

---

64 "The Killers—Jenny Was a Friend of Mine," Genius, n.d., https://genius.com/The-killers-jenny-was-a-friend-of-mine-lyrics.

There ain't no getting back this time

GenAI, I thought you were a friend of mine

Now come on, oh, come on, oh, come on

Oh, come on

Now tell me

What I wanna know!

I asked my friend if he AI'd

What a surprise

A sports analogy

A football pic

A team on each side

With missing body parts

Teams all mixed,

Orange and green

But seven footballs

Now that's just

Flat-out obscene!

Tell us what we wanna know

Oh, come on, oh, come on, oh, come on

And then you whisper in our ear

I'll try to do better this year

So come on, oh, come on, oh, come on

There ain't no getting back this time

GenAI, I thought you were a friend of mine

Oh, come on, oh, come on, oh, come on

Now tell me

What I wanna know!!!

The Reframing of Communication

I've spent this entire chapter talking about communication. How the process of how we talk to each other in the supply chain system needs to be overhauled, because it's just not working.

But let's reframe that a bit. Why isn't it working? What about the system isn't moving in the right direction?

Trust. That's the key right there. Once we have that, communication will improve—I guarantee it. Yes, there will be stumbles along the way, and we know things aren't always going to be perfect. But trust is the best way for us to avoid communication breakdowns. Now we have to get there.

CHAPTER SIX

Rethink Everything

We are farthest apart when we forget we have hearts
Now it's time for us to remember
It's now or never, there's no one better when
We come together

—"COME TOGETHER," TRAPT AND ANOMALY

I spent a lot of time in chapter 5 talking about my friend Ken and the nightclub/warehouse problem that he encountered, and you might be wondering why I did that. Sure, Ken's a nice guy, and he certainly knows his stuff, but why are we talking about the inability of Londoners to find a decent bathroom in a bad part of town?

Ken's skill set is about seeing things not as other people do but as they are. He looks at objects from all sorts of different angles, and because of that, he comes up with solutions that you and I just may not be able to. He's not just a thinker; he's also a *re*thinker—his goal is to look at problems from another perspective.

We need to do exactly that with the global supply chain.

You Can Find Me in the Club

The story that Ken told in the last chapter about the dance club turned music festival is also a great analogy for the internet. Online, you communicate via email or direct messages. At a dance club, you communicate via screaming in excitement or with your lighters. It's all just in the methodology. There's a lot of collaboration going on in both spaces as well. At the festival there's the band, and they work together, and on the internet, well, there's plenty of collaboration to be had there as well.

If you really want to go deep, think about what Meta's doing with the Metaverse and how we'll be using digital avatars to do everything we do on the internet together—including dancing.[65] Now this, in particular, is a great big digital experience experiment, and nobody knows whether or not it's a hit or a miss. But what we do know is the ability to rethink something that we know well—the internet—is being done today. We have the technology.

We didn't start the global supply chain with any of the modern conveniences we have today. We didn't start it with contract negotiation, contract performance, and contract compliance either. What we did was begin with procurement (i.e., we want to get stuff), and then moved on to operations (i.e., we need staff). Inevitably, this all led to frustration. Everything is going wrong everywhere, and this is where we need Ken-type logic. We need to rethink all of that.

---

65 "I Went Clubbing in Virtual Reality: Raves of the Metaverse," PBS, April 7, 2022, https://www.pbs.org/video/i-went-clubbing-in-virtual-reality-raves-of-the-metaverse-zryfsq/.

The Big Dig

Let's put this into another frame of reference: roads. Have you ever been to Boston? New York City? These are areas where the roads were made for getting animals from one place to the next, not four-ton trucks sharing the space with a guy like me who just wants to get a coffee. The infrastructure they built over two hundred years ago still stands today, but it doesn't meet today's demands.

This is the global supply chain in a nutshell. It was built an eternity ago from today's technological perspective. If it were a city, it would make Boston and New York look like well-organized structures compared with the fragmented and disorganized mess we have today. Customers, suppliers, and partners all take similar journeys, but the way each one does it is so different. We can communicate with each other, sure. But transforming those conversations into actions? Into system transactions? Good luck with that.

Part of the problem is of our own making, and that goes back to the internet. It seems like every other day I get an email saying somebody's data centers were hatched, and now I have a free three-month trial for Norton LifeLock because someone in their IT department used the password "password123" for their servers. As a result, we do a lot to try to protect our data, which, frankly, we should. But that also means we're building walls between us and everyone else. We're stuck in a message communication traffic jam.

Plus, there are very few off-ramps, or ways to share information. Email, voice, data entry, and yes, even faxes are still in play, which means that, in short, we made humans the systems interface. There's no way to penetrate those cybersecurity barriers, even if we need to for completely legitimate reasons. It's like we can't find a way out of the road we're on. There's no GPS in the world that can navigate the tangled mess of human and system interactions we have today.

Middle (of No) Ware™

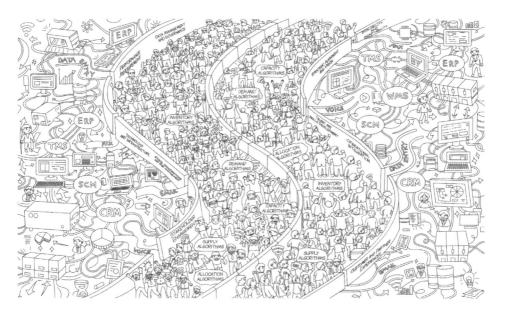

C'mon. We can do better than this.

So let's do that strategic rethink and move things forward instead of sitting here stuck in traffic. And let's begin with one of the most daunting tasks: cyber.

Hard Pass

There's a scenario I've seen play out countless times over the years in enterprises worldwide. A department—doesn't matter which one—discovers a new SaaS platform that can do something absolutely transformational for them. For the sake of this example, let's say it's great at transportation and logistics.

But there's a catch: In order for this platform to be truly great, it must be connected to upstream data and the company's existing enterprise resource planning (ERP) or warehouse management system (WMS). That requires a meeting with the chief of cybersecurity for the company and their team to review the integration requests. Everyone gathers in a room on that fateful day. They sit, the department nervous and anxious. It's quick chitchat at the start until the chief walks in, then a hush comes over the room.

He sits, looks at the head of the department, and says, "No." Then gets up and walks out, and that's the end of that.

Of course, the answer was clear to any observer from the start. Integrations are not allowed with an ERP or WMS ever. Period. Full stop. Get out.

Why? Security, of course. Any integration that you add into a system is a potential point of entry for a hacker or other person with malicious intent. When asked, the chief would answer something such as "Because it's our policy," or "Because it's aligned with our cyber strategy," or another relatively polite way to tell the asker to pound sand.

This practice, of course, is due for a rethink.

Obviously, cybersecurity is important. I don't want to get any more of those emails, and I'm sure nobody else does either. But if you start to look at each scenario a little bit differently, such that you can begin to visualize the real-world impacts and gains that we can achieve, it becomes pretty powerful—particularly when we share these insights with our partners and customers. As I laid out in chapter 4, by Forestreaming™ these shifting supply and demand signals, we maximize our ability to adapt. That requires shared information.

I believe we should focus on certain strategies first. This will maximize our impact overall and give us further inroads for more gains over time. While all of these strategies will need to be adjusted to emphasize inclusivity, collaboration, and cocreation, it also gives us a path forward.

These ten strategies are where we should start. Are they a little messy? Absolutely, but in the next chapter, I will guide you in the right direction. So with that in mind, let's lay these out so we're all on the same page.

1. Build a Strategic Alignment and Vision

Speaking of getting everyone on the same page, everything starts with strategic alignment and vision. This is where all the parties involved align, and that way they can create a shared vision for AI. It'll incorporate input from customers and partners, and that way it hits everyone's needs and expectations. Once that's done, you'll work with those same folks to create objectives for the new AI system. Things such as data sensitivity and privacy are obvious marks to hit, but you've also got things such as confidentiality agreements and the like. Basically, by bringing everyone into the fold, you're making sure everyone bonds and feels like they're a part of things. And look, all of this is based on trust, right? By starting with a strategic alignment and vision, you're making sure there's a solid foundation for you to build this tower of trust.

2. Get Stakeholders Engaged

Now while that first part is the core team, there will be other stakeholders in the process, and you need to get them engaged. I'm talking about things such as inclusive communication practices, having joint workshops so everyone can provide feedback, and creating methods of communication that are secure and discrete. Privacy and security are absolutely critical, and you don't want a wrench thrown in the works because someone was using the wrong messaging system. Oh, and to build that trust even further, make sure that any data usage information is completely transparent. Like, completely. You want there to be no questions about anything, because that trust is sacrosanct.

3. Sew Up Data Management and Governance

Speaking of, let's get into data management and governance. What I'm proposing means mixing data from multiple sources, and not everyone is going to be kosher with that, which is why I'm using so many construction metaphors in relation to trust. Your data strategy— the way you store, organize, and manage information—has to be agreed upon by everyone with a collaborative governance structure. Every party has a stake in this, so they all should have people who oversee data use and make sure the appropriate AI ethics concerns are addressed. Conversely, whoever has access to that information also needs to be limited based on their roles. The IT person doesn't need to know all of the minutiae, and your widget rep doesn't need to know the data you get from your dongle rep. Everyone gets a slice, but not everyone gets the whole pie.

4. Ensure Technology and Systems Interoperability

Technology is also going to play a huge role in this whole thing, but that's probably pretty obvious at this point. If you've ever had an ERP or just worked within one, you know how tricky it can be to get one ERP to play with another. Now you may not have any ERPs involved, but no matter what, this AI system that you create has to work with other groups and their technology. You need interoperability. That way all the data that's shared is done so seamlessly. You'll have some shared platforms that everyone uses, and of course, all sensitive data should be encrypted so the bad guys can't get it. Secure APIs help with that too. That way the data is kept confidential even when new applications are added to the mix.

5. Create Joint Training Programs

There's gonna be a lot of folks involved in this whole thing, and you know what that means: training. Yes, you're going to get all of your teams together for a real bonding session full of trust falls and the like but maybe minus the campfire. Seriously, though, your people and everyone else's people will have joint training programs so everyone knows how to do things the same way. This will build a community of best practices, where people become AI experts, and all involved learn the right and wrong ways to do things. There will be data protection training, too, and maybe you can even create a certification program for those who complete the work. If not, encourage bringing on already certified professionals, whether it's in data protection, cybersecurity, or something else entirely, so your group has some street cred.

6. Design Structures for Ethical Considerations and Risk Management

One of the things that always gets in the way in these situations is other people's opinions, particularly when it comes to ethics and how risky they want to be. This is why committees exist, and you should build one that's inclusive to all partners and stakeholders. This way you could build your own ethical standards that everyone can agree with, and make sure you all have the same risk assessment protocols in place. This is also where you can build your ethical AI framework, the one with all the super tight data protection standards, and create risk mitigation plans to prepare for the unexpected—or hacks.

7. Create Operational Integration

Everyone is going to be working together, and that means you're going to have to change some of the things you're doing. Your business processes have to be rebuilt, and you should work with your customers and partners so the AI solutions you're offering work with what they need. You can set them up on pilot projects, for example. Let them test the AI waters before you dive into them headfirst. And then once things are working the way you like, make sure you're conducting regular audits so vulnerabilities are found before they become a problem.

8. Measure Your Performance

Boy, we all love our metrics and KPIs, don't we? Well, we have them for a reason, and your KPIs should match what your partner uses as well. These shared KPIs will determine how successful your AI initiatives are, from multiple perspectives. Think about your customers, partners, and organizations. When there are problems, have a joint review session so you can tweak and tune issues before they become too big. Create security metrics so you can figure out how effective your systems are, and again, make sure to do regular reviews of everything. Nothing stays perfect forever, and what may seem bulletproof today could be leaky as a sieve tomorrow. Audits help plug those holes.

9. Have Amazing Customer and Partner Experiences

We all work better when we work together. Now you need to integrate AI into the mix, and make sure you're adding value to everyone at the table. One way to do this is through a joint value proposition, which highlights the good things you're going to do through your system. But for it to be truly effective, you should have some kind of feedback mechanism. Something that gives you a way to receive info from your people so you can do more of that tweaking and tuning I love to talk about.

10. Make Sure Everything Is Scalable and Adaptable

Remember back in number eight how I said everything isn't perfect forever? Yeah, this applies to your AI system too. It's gotta be scalable. There may come a time when you decide to pull in another stakeholder or partner into the project. Can you do that? Only if you've built the system that way from the beginning. And what if something goes south? Adapt and change, buddy. Adjust as threats grow and use adaptive risk management strategies when things happen, not four years later.

But Wait, There's More

That's not all. If you want extra credit, start thinking about things such as using blockchain technology to keep your data secure and transparent. Or you can make sure all data is anonymized so privacy is kept paramount. And also, there's multifactor authentication, or MFA. You know how sometimes you have to use an app to provide a number so your computer knows it's you? That and other biometric security options are really good ideas to keep everything locked up.

Back to the Party

We made the global supply chain as complex as it is today for a ton of reasons, but it's time for us to make a big change. The next stage has to be going direct-to-doorstep with our customers, and for this to happen, we have to enter our next Silent Shift™: apply a new way of thinking to our much more complex global supply businesses at scale to adapt to this new world. We need to rethink everything.

In Ken's story, the one about the nightclub née rock festival, you learned how something meant to be simple became much more complex. An environment designed for people to party in a safe space became a problem once people figured out how to make money on it. That led to crime, and without rethinking the problem, it would have just gotten worse.

The global supply chain has the same history, particularly once the internet was introduced into the system. What started out as a way to get goods from one person to another has, thanks to the profit motive, become a place where crime and theft can take place regularly. That means more cybersecurity, strategies, policies, regulations, and audits—a whole ton of stuff that just bogs everything down.

The internet was supposed to be akin to a music festival, but once it became a place to make money, the knives came out.

To change these things for the better, we have to rethink it all. And one of the ways we're going to do that is through efficiency. We're going to get better at communicating and exchanging ideas and information, and we're going to do it together. After all, it's now or never. There's no one better when we come together.

CHAPTER SEVEN

Improve Efficiency

Maybe he'll see a little better set of days.

—"EVEN FLOW," PEARL JAM

I spent a good portion of the introduction to this book talking about my jaded views on education when I was growing up. This is an opinion that I have obviously evolved from, but back in my pre-eighteen years, I had tons of free time on my hands.

I wasn't reading the things I was told to read for book reports and the like, obviously. Instead, I created an essay formula that could fool even today's AI scanners. Back then the idea was to write an introduction, then the body paragraphs, and finally the conclusion. To me that read as follows:

1. Tell them what you're going to tell them

2. Tell them

3. Tell them that you've told them

You're given a question, right? So the first step is to tell the reader that you have received, acknowledged, and understood their question. This is the introduction. Then the body is the answer. For that, I needed to get to class ten minutes early so I could gather some quick character and story facts from the classmates who actually had read the book. And the conclusion just reaffirms that you accomplished the task. Easy.

(It turns out this is also how Aristotle taught people public speaking.[66] Great minds think alike, I guess.)

I couldn't be bothered with tests either. That was all too subjective to me. I just couldn't connect those dots, and the result was finding myself being excessively bored.

Instead of focusing on my schoolwork, I would fiddle and tinker with whatever thing happened to be in front of me at that moment. If the teacher handed me a piece of paper, it could become an instant airplane—or maybe a football. But sometimes crazier things would happen.

I've always had a deeply personal connection to the concept of infinity. I'm not sure exactly what it is, but this idea percolates in my brain constantly. I think it's why my favorite number is eight, as it's a symbolic representation of the proper symbol for infinity, just standing up rather than lying down.

One day, around Christmastime, when I was much younger, one of my teachers had us create decorations from paper. I'm a leftie, and I hate those giant left-handed pencils and scissors, so instead of messing about with cutting something, I saw these precut strips of paper in the corner, and I grabbed a bunch to work with.

Looking around the classroom, I saw several of my classmates using scotch tape and those paper strips to create a loop. Then they

---

66   John Baldoni, "Give a Great Speech: 3 Tips from Aristotle," *Inc.*, May 4, 2012, https://www.inc.com/john-baldoni/deliver-a-great-speech-aristotle-three-tips.html.

would loop the next paper strip into the first, creating another link in their decorative chain.

Now this wasn't my style. After all, my folks had already decorated the house with all of my favorite stuff, so I had no interest in creating some kind of paper chain. But something about the material itself did interest me.

What else could I do with this flat, rectangular shape? Yes, I could do the chain thing, but could I come up with something new?

I tried folding the paper, and that created some interesting three-dimensional shapes. But the pieces weren't long enough to create a decently sized square or triangle. OK, scratch that off the list.

But what about making my favorite number? Could I shape the paper into the number eight?

Well, the paper wasn't long enough, so after taping a couple of strips together end to end, I realized I could make it happen. Kinda. All I had to do was twist the paper the right direction and then tape the two ends together. There it was, and I was excited.

I had started with these simple strips of paper, and next thing I knew, I had what resembled my old Tyco slot car race track with what appeared to be an infinite surface.

Wait, was that right? It made no sense, but as I traced the surface of the paper digit with my finger, starting on what was the top surface, it eventually glided to the bottom surface and back to the top without ever leaving the piece of paper. How was that possible?

(Seriously, try it, and see what I mean. Take a strip of paper, twist it once, and then connect the ends. If you glide your fingertip along the surface, you'll see what I'm talking about.)

It was an amazing discovery to my young self, but like most things, it faded away into my memory palace, never to be seen again.

Well, until recently, anyway.

Kids Love Chains

I've dedicated over thirty years of my professional life to bringing meaningful improvement to the world of global supply chain management. But that word—chain—causes me to cringe every time.

Even so, I use it all the time, mainly because keyword experts and the like tell me it's important. I should speak the way humanity speaks today instead of talking about the future like it's the present.

Why do I have a problem with the concept of chains as in supply chain?

Kids love chains. They're a simple enough design to create with strips of paper and a little bit of scotch tape. But look at each link. It's alone. Solitary. Forced to stay in a stable set of relationships, with one, maybe two connections. Why is that kind of isolationist perspective the optimal strategy for global supply?

I was talking to a friend of mine once about it and shared my paper garland story as well, and he immediately related to it. His name is Jon McCutcheon, and he pointed out that what I had created at that young age is a Möbius strip.

Now I, obviously, was not the person who discovered the Möbius strip. That would be Johann Benedict Listing and August Ferdinand Möbius back in 1858.[67] It also, according to Tony Stark in 2019's *Avengers: Endgame,* is the solution to time travel.[68]

But besides fictional accounts depicted by Robert Downey Jr., the Möbius strip is also the subject of an article that Jon shared with

---

67   "Möbius Strip," Wikipedia, accessed June 15, 2024, https://en.wikipedia.org/wiki/M%C3%B6bius_strip.

68   Filmey Box, "Tony Stark Figures Out Time Travel Scene | Avengers Endgame (2019) IMAX Movie Clip HD 4K," July 27, 2022, https://www.youtube.com/watch?v=uKndgvlu5MY.

me: "The Timeless Journey of the Möbius Strip" by Serena Alagappan. In it, she shares something that hit me pretty hard:

> There's a depth to the image that reminds you to reduce, reuse and recycle. It is not just a circular action; it's dynamic. The symbol seeks to represent the three interdependent aspects of a sustainable loop: the collection of materials to be recycled, the manufacturing of recycled materials into new products, and the purchase and use of the products made from recycled materials. Each arrow pleats and pivots itself, as all three arrows pursue and power one another.[69]

This got me thinking about global supply, as most things do. The article mentions how some manufacturers use a Möbius strip for a conveyor belt because it extends the belt's overall life. The same rationale could be applied to our supply chain, and it was part of what became my vision of the future of global supply.

The Möbius Strip of Global Supply

Imagine a future where you receive demand signals. Jim in Toronto needs pencils, or Frank in St. Louis wants a new trash can. This triggers you to act, so then you send those signals in one direction along your supply flow (notice that I didn't say "chain"), and as those signals are transformed into supply, they're then transported to your

---

69   Serena Alagappan, "The Timeless Journey of the Möbius Strip," *Scientific American*, February 20, 2024, https://www.scientificamerican.com/article/the-timeless-journey-of-the-moebius-strip/.

customers, who further transform them into greater demand. There you have it: the Möbius strip of global supply.

The Möbius Strip of Global Supply

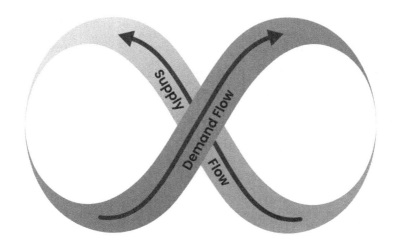

On its surface this seems like a pipe dream. We've got decades, if not centuries, of basic supply chain theory built into our brains. It works. It's not glorious, and sometimes it's a little (or a lot) wonky. But whatever. It works, right? Why change? People hate change.

Sure, you could take that angle. For me, though, I look at it differently: change is good. And in this case, we can make this change today. Right now. Here's how you do it:

1. Categorize your internal and external stakeholders.

2. Identify the data that you could get from them faster, or even at all.

3. Consider the data they would also like to get from you.

4. Score the potential impact on business performance, efficiency, etc. (high/medium/low).

5. Identify the blockers people may cite as why we couldn't achieve this.

6. Start the conversations with "What if we could …"

If you're this far into the book, then you know about the concept of Forestreaming™, which I introduced back in chapter 4. For that to be successful, you need to engage in global supply signal sharing. To do this, you talk to people, share ideas, and come up with plans to make things work better.

And since you know change is coming, take the best pathway to your bigger future by learning and adapting from the front, as opposed to sitting in the back and passively waiting for your turn on the new system.

Disconnected Conversations™ Drive Bullwhips
Every Delayed Supply / Demand Has Growing Adverse Effect Downstream

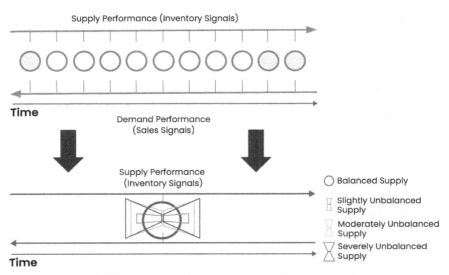

Now it's not going to be easy. There is no linear path to get from where we are now to where we could be in the future. But this is an "us" thing; we can't go at this alone. The key to Forestreaming™ is shared information. You need collaboration from your best customers, suppliers, and transport partners. And you need to know that each of those groups is at its own point along the path to developing or participating in AI ecosystems™. How do you know where everyone sits on that chain?

The Viking Compass

If you've got a smartphone, you have access to a compass. While this isn't something I pull out on a regular basis, I never want to take this technology for granted. At one time in history, the magnetic compass was a big deal. It was how people navigated the globe or figured out how to get back home if they were lost in the woods. They didn't just have to navigate by the stars anymore; they could use something anytime, in any place.

Then there are the Vikings. The Viking Age was roughly 800–1050 CE,[70] and those folks did a lot of sailing. They went as far as North America and all by boat, which is pretty impressive considering the times. From what we know, they used a device called the Uunartoq disc[71] to navigate the open seas.

Now we're never going to know what actually happened, but right now the running theory is they used this disc like a sundial. The

---

70   "The Viking Age," National Museum of Denmark, n.d., https://en.natmus.dk/historical-knowledge/denmark/prehistoric-period-until-1050-ad/the-viking-age/.

71   Laura Poppick, "Forget GPS: Medieval Compass Guided Vikings After Sunset," Livescience, March 26, 2014, https://www.livescience.com/44366-vikings-sun-compass-after-sunset.html.

sun would cast its light down onto the disc, and it would project a shadow in a direction that they would use for navigation. Easy, right?

But what about sailing at night? And have you ever been to Norway? It's not exactly Phoenix, Arizona, where 85 percent of the year, it's sunny for roughly 310.25 days.[72] No, Oslo, Norway, gets about 1,668 *hours* of sunlight a year,[73] which works out to 69.5 days. How are they supposed to use a sundial if there's no sun?

So that's the other weird part. It turns out they may have used crystals. According to an article in Live Science,

> To use the crystal, the Vikings would have held the stone up to the center of the sky (from their perspective). When sunlight hits the crystal, that light gets polarized and broken into an "ordinary" and an "extraordinary" beam.[74]
>
> On a clear day, the Vikings would have rotated the crystal until the two beams lined up. Since these two beams line up and have the same brightness at only one angle, by noting where the sun is when this happens the Vikings could establish a reference point that could be used even when the sun wasn't visible.[75]

72 Teresa Bitler, "It's Always Sunny: 25 Sunniest Cities in the U.S.," Moving.Com (blog), June 3, 2022, https://www.moving.com/tips/sunniest-cities-us/.

73 "Average Sunshine a Year at Cities in Europe," Current Results, n.d., https://www.currentresults.com/Weather/Europe/Cities/sunshine-annual-average.php.

74 Jennifer Welsh, "'Magic' Viking Sunstone Just Natural Crystal," Livescience, November 1, 2011, https://www.livescience.com/16831-viking-sunstone-crystal-compass.html.

75 Ibid.

How crazy is that? The Vikings had a way to navigate by the sun even when the sun wasn't visible, and they used it to travel regularly to Greenland and occasionally to North America. That's absolutely nuts.

This compass, and the compass overall, was a huge breakthrough in world travel. Prior to this, sailors could use the stars, but there weren't a lot of other reliable options, particularly for long distances, that didn't involve just following the coast. It was revolutionary and completely changed the game.

But you didn't buy this book to learn about the Vikings (although if you did, you get ten extra points), so why am I bringing it up? Because what the world of global supply needs is a compass. A way to point it in a direction because right now we're rudderless. Nobody is leading the ship, and we have no idea where we need to go.

Your company needs something similar. You need your own North Star to point toward to navigate you where you need to be. That AI Ecosystems Readiness Flow™ is that star, and the Assessment is a big part of that process.

So let's do that now. Let's put this all into perspective and figure out how to get the global supply chain on the right track.

Preparing for the Digital Future

This, right here, is our compass.

AI Ecosystems Readiness Flow™

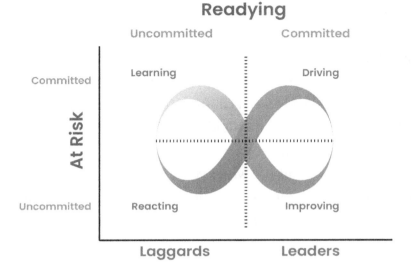

It's a tool I've called the AI Ecosystems Readiness Flow™, and it combines the concept of the compass with the flow of a Möbius strip. This is the precursor to the AI Ecosystems™ Readiness Assessment, which is an actual test you can take on my website—but more on that shortly.

Let's start by laying this out into quadrants. In the northeast corner, there is the Driving quadrant. This is where you want to be in an ideal world. You've finished all of the questions in the Assessment, and you want as many of those answers in that area as possible.

Next, in the southeast quadrant is Improving. Here, you're going in the right direction, which is toward the Driving area, but you're not quite there yet. There's room for improvement—hence the name.

In the northwest corner is Learning, and that's suboptimal. At this point you're not quite ready to move forward in the way you need to go, but at least you know there are issues to address.

Where you really don't want to be is in the southwest quadrant, because that's Reacting. If you're just reacting to the world around you as it all happens, you're never going to get anywhere. You need to make a full stop and cease all efforts facing that direction to have any chance of being an industry leader and implementing the kinds of concepts needed for an AI ecosystem.

So how do you find out where you're at on the compass with your business? The easy answer is to take a test of some kind. Figure out where people stand and how you fit into that equation. If only there was an option.

An Introduction to AI Ecosystems™ Readiness Assessment

If you're in the global supply chain world, then you know we're battling increasing pressure to enhance visibility and transparency, as well as our usual job of delivering cargo. To do that, we need to invest more in technology, which isn't cheap. Oh, and we need to have more competitive pricing, which means we may not take in as much money. You can see the push and pull here.

When you dig deeper into the overall global supply chain, you see the market dynamics that created the Silent Shift™. This force has reshaped and will continue to change the way global supply design functions, just like the way water will carve out a new path for a stream.

And just like that stream, things are ebbing and flowing constantly, putting more strain on different areas. As markets increase in volatility, the Silent Shift™ becomes more volatile. Everyone that's caught in the middle, as one stage of the shift gives way to the next, faces an uncertain future. But they all have one thing in common, which is their relatively equal footing. Basically, they have to digitize their systems or die.

But why?

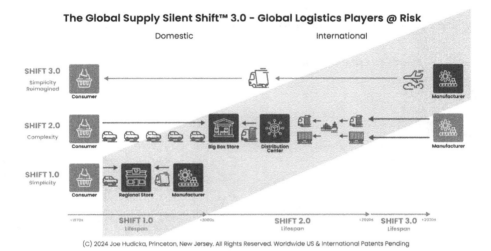

The Global Supply Silent Shift™ 3.0 – Global Logistics Players @ Risk

(C) 2024 Joe Hudicka, Princeton, New Jersey. All Rights Reserved. Worldwide US & International Patents Pending

Whenever there is change, there will be a resistance to that force. The Silent Shift™ is a constant state of change that lurks in the background, invisible to everyone but those who know what to look for. There's no way to predict where it will move and go. At least there isn't as a human being.

Digitalization not only bridges that gap but also provides a fast track to creating more value from less resources. This can help offset the demand for transparency and lower pricing, because you're able to do more with what you have. Yes, the digitalization will cost some money up front, but it will save overall. By delivering a higher value, you will get greater revenues. And when your business processes are fully optimized, you'll be able to maximize your profitability in virtually any market conditions.

To do so requires you to be able to see those invisible Silent Shift™ moments faster than your competitors. Then you have to take those messages and be able to do something with them; synthesize the information from mere data and information to something you can take action on. It allows you to make decisions faster and react accordingly.

This is Forestreaming™, just like we discussed two chapters ago, and it's a real-time replacement for twentieth-century forecasting methods.

FORESTREAM™ – Adaptive Forecasting Shapes the FUTURE

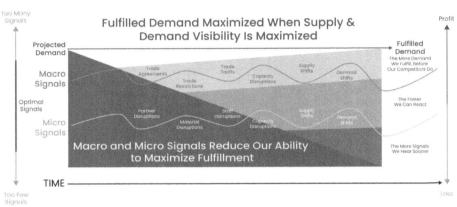

But how do you start making that digital transformation? With the previously teased AI Ecosystems™ Readiness Assessment.

AI Ecosystems™ Readiness Assessment

Our AI Ecosystems™ Readiness Assessment is your starting point. You answer a few questions about your business, and the results you get back show how ready you are to integrate an AI ecosystem™ into your existing flow.

Some of you reading this book are ready. Like, really ready. You've got the pumps primed, and you want to dive right in. Others might be afraid of what's coming. Change is scary; we get it. And so your Assessment might reflect that reality, and that's OK.

You can start right now by scanning the QR code below to take the Assessment.

www.joehudicka.com/assessment

Once you know where you stand, you can know how to move forward.

Parody Plays

Way back in the last chapter, I put together a parody song called "GenAI Was a Friend of Mine," and I really enjoyed that process. I'm obviously very much a music person, and since then I've created a few more of those songs just for fun.

So what I did was create what I'm calling the Parody Supply Chain. We start with a concept, then it moves to song selection, lyrics, music composition, vocal composition, recording, design, production, and finally, completed parody videos. In fact, we've got two more in the hopper ready to go.

How do you get to them? Easy. You can find them by scanning the QR code below.

www.joehudicka.com/parody-supply-chain

We're not done yet either. We're going to continue making these kinds of parodies until, well, we don't want to anymore.
So if you're looking to spend a little bit more time on the fun side of things, this is what you need.

Beginning Your Digital Transformation

Have you ever been to Disneyland or Disney World? They had this thing called the Lightning Lane. Basically, it was a way for you to kind of cut in line for a ride; that way you didn't have to sit for hours in the heat, listening to your child complain about getting more popcorn.

Our AI Ecosystems™ Readiness Assessment is just like that, but without the potential for nausea and kernels stuck in your teeth. It's how you get from where you are today to that digital future, and even though it sounds like a tough transition, it's just a part of evolution.

After all, every ecosystem changes over time. Sometimes that shift happens between different ecosystems, too, and every participant can influence how they react to those changes. We are all empowered to control our evolution.

The AI Ecosystems Flow™ is a model that we designed through our study of the global supply chain, but you can adapt it to work with any industry. It's a powerful tool, particularly at this moment.

It's not hyperbole to say that the implementation of AI into the global supply chain could be revolutionary. Look at where the industry is at now: old-school technologies, a lack of communication, and twisted economics. When COVID-19 hit, everyone was taken by surprise, and the supply chain became international news because of how broken it really was.

We can't let that happen again. The global supply chain *has* to evolve. It has to get better to create greater resistance to events such as COVID-19 and whatever else gets thrown our way.

This is where the AI Ecosystems Flow™ provides solutions. It measures an organization, along with its concern and desire to embrace innovation and digitally transform the following three primary drivers of supply chain businesses:

1. Contract negotiation

2. Contract performance

3. Contract compliance

You can then leverage that data to figure out a path forward.

In this Assessment we observe key critical success factors that can directly influence your company's current state of readiness shift toward the new digital world.

Are you prepared today? Probably not. But *how* unprepared are you?

That's the kind of things we're able to discover through the AI Ecosystems Flow™. It has four quadrants, each characterizing an organization's ability to adapt to current conditions, starting in the lower left and rising in the form of an infinite cycle, and there's a visual that I shared just a few pages ago.

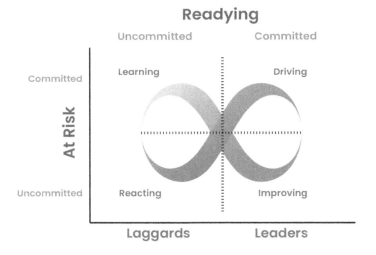

AI Ecosystems Readiness Flow™

Let's take a moment to break down each of these quadrants, working in a zigzag fashion.

Reacting

Reacting is in the lower left corner. Sometimes an organization ends up finding itself in the middle of a crisis because it didn't anticipate certain market conditions, and it has to develop its strategy on the fly. But more commonly, these same companies become reactive because they've become stagnant; they assume that no market condition could change what they're doing and therefore don't do anything. Problem is, there is a need for change, and they have refused to provide the resources to their employees to address the future.

Learning

First up, as we go counterclockwise, is Learning in the top left corner. An organization shifts into the learning stage once they've accepted certain changes in their situation. Adverse conditions push change, and the company then researches possible methods and resources for how they can move forward. They understand that they have to change but have yet to provide the resources they need to address the future.

Improving

In the lower right-hand corner, there is Improving. Once a company has gained enough support to move forward with their Learning insights, and they have a strong leader who is willing to execute, they start to improve. While they may not have actually accepted there's a reason for change, they have given their employees the resources they need to begin exploring new ideas.

Driving

Finally, in the top right corner is Driving. In our world organizations typically aspire to be in this state. This is where you have both a clear direction for where you're going and the resources at hand to be able to execute when you want to grow. The downside here is that sometimes Driving leads to reacting. And sometimes that reacting may be done without any proactive exploration of new market capabilities. Basically, it can mean that you're jumping into the water with both feet instead of checking to see if the surface is frozen or not. While that may make for a funny YouTube video, it can be disastrous for your business.

So with that in mind, how do you use that to your advantage?

Leveraging Flow

The AI Ecosystems Flow™ can be used as a communication tool to weigh the success factors that impact your ability to complete a digital transformation of your global supply transportation and logistics. We've looked at these key factors for the past thirty years and done so with a wide variety of different supply chain participants. We have looked at everyone from manufacturers and shippers (in the 1PL category[76]) to carriers (2PL), freight forwarders (3PL), and wholesale traders and sourcing specialists (4PL).

Better yet, our research team has prepared helpful insights on each one of those key critical success factors and the impact that each one is likely to have on your overall digital transformation readiness. Your overall assessment score is then weighted based on our industry observations to scale higher impact factors compared with others. And in the end, your data is only shared with you and the people of EvenFlow. You and your company's confidentiality is assured.

The result of all this is to make sure that the amount of energy you put into your business is equaled on the way out. What we want to do is improve efficiency so that you're not working harder than you need to.

It's about creating an EvenFlow. And that's what we do.

Of course, to really make sure things flow properly, we need to ensure everyone is on the same page. And that, of course, takes trust.

---

76   Hadleigh Reid, "Comparing Logistics Providers—the Main Differences between a 1PL, 2PL, 3PL, 4PL, and 5PL," DCL Logistics, May 9, 2024, https://dclcorp.com/blog/3pl/difference-between-1pl-2pl-3pl-4pl-5pl/.

CHAPTER EIGHT

Earn Trust

Won't you tell me something true?

—"ELEVATION," U2

So here we are, two-thirds of the way through the book, and I still haven't really told you what an AI ecosystem is. And it's appropriate here, in the chapter about building trust, that we start out talking about something that does not currently engender a lot of trust but will soon.

Let's start off by talking about what's not an AI ecosystem, and that's the AI models that you're the most familiar with today. These large language models (LLMs) can be used by anyone.

Today, you can pop onto the ChatGPT website and ask it whatever you like. It's a pretty neat trick.

But this kind of AI is completely public. It was trained on data from the web, and anything you enter into it is also fair game for them to use for further training. Basically, if you don't want your information to be public, you probably shouldn't use it.

Public LLMs are high risk and low reward.

This is where a chart would be handy, which is why it's very convenient that I have one.

The AI Ecosystems (R)evolution™

Permissioned Data Sets Maximize Returns for You, Your Customers & Your Partners

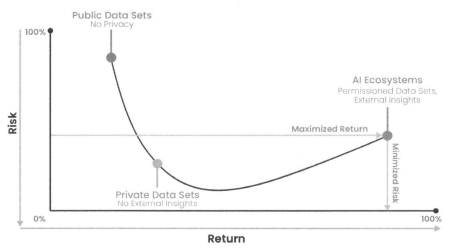

© 2024 Joe Hudicka, Princeton, New Jersey. All Rights Reserved.
Worldwide US & International Patents Pending

Then we get into private AI silos. These are sometimes referred to as the "private pile," meaning that the only thing that feeds these AI models is your own data. It's private, and nobody else has access to it.

While this sounds great, public LLMs have so much data that they seemingly don't have enough. At one point Meta, the parent company of Facebook and Instagram, considered buying Simon & Schuster, the publishing company, just so they could have more data to train their model.[77]

---

77   Cade Metz et al., "How Tech Giants Cut Corners to Harvest Data for AI," *New York Times*, April 6, 2024, https://www.nytimes.com/2024/04/06/technology/tech-giants-harvest-data-artificial-intelligence.html?searchResultPosition=13.

Chances are pretty good that your company doesn't have more data to train on than the entirety of the internet plus a publishing house, so it is possible that you won't get the kind of results you want.

That said, you will get more specific results, and that's probably a win. Your data is also completely yours, so you don't have to worry about people getting your information as a result when they're using something such as ChatGPT.

In this case, you get a little bit better return and much less risk.

But there is a third option, and it's one that is just on the horizon. I'm calling it the AI ecosystem. In this case, you do have publicly traded data, but it's only the base. This is what helps you with being able to query using natural language and the ability to ask it questions in tandem with your own.

The second part, though, is critical. For this, you have data sets that can only be accessed by permission. It's like you have your own ChatGPT/Bard/Gemini, and it uses your data but has all of the strength of a public LLM.

There's a reason why this is necessary. Today, if you were to ask someone in the C-suite if you could use an AI product, it would be a flat, "No." And it's understandable why. You're asking if you can input the company's private data into a system that hoovers up information. That's a hard pass from me, dog.

But the future, as I've hammered home a million times so far, is an AI ecosystem. A way for your data to do the work of tons of employees and forecast (or Forestream™) things that nobody short of a psychic could predict.

On top of that, AI systems today take a lot of power. There's a bunch of hardware required, too, and it can get complicated. Nobody wants their IT department dealing with that. I mean, imagine how many story points that would be.

Realistically, though, this isn't going to be an IT department thing. Just like Microsoft Azure and Amazon AWS, you'll probably be able to outsource this somewhere. But you still need to know your data is cordoned off from everyone else's, and assuming that all comes to play, you're golden.

What all that means is you will have your own siloed AI ecosystem™, and with that you'll be able to build up a healthy data querying system. And one, more importantly, that's built on trust.

It's Foundational

Here's the thing: trust is earned, not given.

You know this because you're a human being walking this Earth. You've met untrustworthy people before, or you've discovered that you can't trust a piece of technology because it keeps failing. But you know what trust is because you've seen it succeed and fall flat. We all have; it's part of the human condition.

The supply chain is built on that trust. Each link in that chain is trusting that the person they need stuff from will deliver, and you have someone who is trusting you to deliver it to them.

Thing is, though, we don't *actually* trust each other. Not like family does. If you were my brother, sure, I'd trust you with the keys to my new car. Just bring it back with a full tank. But would I loan someone in the supply chain a pencil? Probably not. They might be the competition, after all.

We need to build that trust; otherwise, this all will continue moving as it does today, which is to say OK but not great. There is definitely room for improvement.

I think we need to break this down into the three areas of trust where we're lacking the most in supply chain: data, technology, and relationships.

Trust in Your Data

Trust in your data means knowing that the information you have at hand is good data—it's accurate and correct. If it's not, then it's worthless.

That sounds harsh, but it's true. You could have decades of information stored on hard drives, but if it was all inputted manually by Phyllis from accounting (or Bob from sales, I'm not picky), then it's untrustworthy and therefore worthless.

You need clean data. Information that's super accurate and able to be trusted. But let me take you way back to chapter 3 and my buddy Guido Burger. I summed it up, but here are his words:

> "Today, we have a supply chain, which is really very much controlled by ERP systems. So they get an order in. They process the order. We look at all the orders that we got in the past. Now we are already [working with] historic data. And then we try to manage our supplier somehow, but we don't get all the supplier subsidiaries in one bucket."

Guido continued, "We have a ton of data in supply chain that we really can't trust, of course. It's manual data entered in a system, [with] maybe [a] wrong typo or whatever. It's scanned information, which is not uploaded yet or whatever it is. So the data that we have is siloed, and it's sometimes not in a quality that we need."

This is the first part of the trust problem that we have within the supply chain as it stands, and it's a tough one to get past. How do you correct information that's potentially decades old? How do you get the type of data that you need today that you didn't think you required years ago?

Trust in Your Tech

Then there's your technology. Today, we're talking all about AI and its ability to take data sets and turn it into relevant information that we can query using natural language. But it wasn't that long ago that the World Wide Web was a big deal, and we were all trying to grab our first domain names. Time marches on, as does technology. And now, more than ever, you have to trust that it works.

Let's start with the hardware side of things. Your business may have racks of servers scattered across the globe or have an old Drobo sitting on someone's desktop in Kansas City. Whatever physical hardware you use, whether it's laptops, hard drives, scanning tools, or anything else, this hardware has to do what you need it to do on a reliable basis.

Now I could get all "Old man yells at cloud" about this whole thing (go ahead and check out *The Simpsons* season 13, episode 13[78] for that joke's explanation), but technology used to be made to last decades. Look at refrigerators, for example. One made in the 1950s can still be in operation today with the proper maintenance. Meanwhile, if I buy one from Best Buy tomorrow, it might last me ten years if I'm very, very lucky.

---

78   *The Simpsons*, season 13, episode 13, "The Old Man and the Key," written by Matt Groening, James L. Brooks, and Sam Simon, directed by Jim Reardon and Lance Kramer, aired on March 10, 2002, on IMDb, https://www.imdb.com/title/tt0701252/.

Your tech either has to be just as reliable as an old fridge or have backup, and I think that last part is critical no matter how well the machine works. Having a way to cover yourself when something fails is the way you're able to keep things moving on time. Consider backup in all its forms to be important.

And then there's the software side of tech, but let's be realistic here: we're dealing with AI. Today, as it stands, trusting AI has some good sides and some bad sides. The big issue to consider are hallucinations.

AI Hallucinations

AI hallucinations made big news when a reporter for the *New York Times* had a chatbot try to convince him to leave his wife,[79] and yes, that's a little problematic. But AI hallucinations are a very real thing.[80]

If you're unfamiliar with the concept, let me give you the quick rundown. The average AI chatbot is fed information. Using that information, it's able to respond to questions asked of it using predictive text modeling. Basically, you ask an AI chatbot what color the sky is in London today, and it will respond by determining the response one word at a time.

The information fed to a chatbot typically comes from the internet, and I'm not sure if you've been to that place before, but there's a wide variety of opinions out there. Some of them tend to lean a little risqué, and sometimes that leaves you in a scenario where you're getting romanced by Microsoft's Bing.

---

79   Kevin Roose, "A Conversation with Bing's Chatbot Left Me Deeply Unsettled," *New York Times*, February 16, 2023, https://www.nytimes.com/2023/02/16/technology/bing-chatbot-microsoft-chatgpt.html.

80   "When AI Gets It Wrong: Addressing AI Hallucinations and Bias," MIT Sloan Teaching & Learning Technologies, May 7, 2024, https://mitsloanedtech.mit.edu/ai/basics/addressing-ai-hallucinations-and-bias/.

These types of instances are called hallucinations because that's essentially what the AI is doing. It may output biased or completely fabricated information out at you, and that's tough to deal with. Really, that's tough to trust.

What it comes down to is this is a game of poker, where every card is blind. Having the mechanisms, strategies, and policies in place to be able to share securely and take the permission away when one of these hallucinations pops up is pretty important. But in the end, if we're sharing more and behaving responsibly, we should get better value. And if not, then we stop doing that and find another partner.

Trust in Your Relationships

One of the more critical parts of this layer cake we call global supply is trust with our relationships. One of the things we've talked about again and again is how we need to be more collaborative with the other members of our chain. Remember this chart?

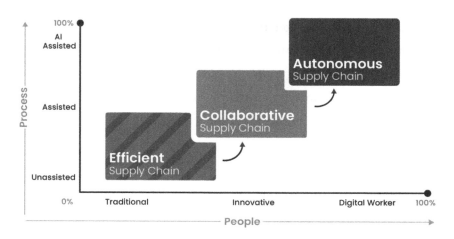

The Flow to Autonomous Supply
The 3 Stages of the AI Ecosystems (R)evolution™

Let's take a moment to explain what you're looking at. You've got your *x*-axis, which is People, scored 0 to 100 percent. Then the *y*-axis is Process, again scored 0 to 100 percent. After taking our AI Ecosystems™ Readiness Assessment, you'll see where you rank on this scale. If you get a perfect score—100, 100—that's our North Star and the goal. If you place anywhere else (which you probably will), you'll have a good idea of what you need to improve on.

This chart also shows you where you're trending, and that's also important. Hopefully, you're trending up. But realistically, the ideal state today, with the way things are at the moment, is around a 50, 50 score. Right there in the middle is the key part: the *Collaborative* Supply Chain. And if we ever want to get to the autonomous supply chain in the future, we need trust and communication.

What I know, you might not know, and you may know things that I don't know. Wouldn't we both be stronger if we shared those details together?

I've got a buddy who tinkers with cars on the weekends, and I was over at his place one day just to hang out and have a few frosty beverages. He was working on this old truck at the time with a custom engine and all that, while I was testing the tensile strength of the thirty-year-old plastic chair that I was sitting in. He pulled out this tool that looked really crazy, so I asked him about it. Turns out that he made it for a very specific purpose. That's right, my friend just made his own tool. It was essentially a normal wrench that had been cut and bent in such a way that it would allow him access to a particular part that he couldn't get with something bought off the shelf. It was amazing.

Car people have all sorts of tricks like that, and they're usually passed on from one person to the next while a glass bottle of something foamy is sitting atop a stack of tires. We in the global supply chain have those same kinds of tips, but we don't share them with each other. Instead, we hoard them like someone's going to steal them from us.

Here's an example. Some companies build buying networks for transportation. The idea is if a group of companies forms a collective, they can get larger volumes and negotiate bigger discounts. If any of the network's members sees their own demand decline, their peers often get even more of a discount, simply because they take the additional commitment off the other company's hands. We see this even more outside of networks, too, because the pressure of contracted commitments is even greater on a company that stands alone, particularly if they cannot fulfill their buying obligations.

But in all those situations, only one group gets the benefits. But we *all* have those tips. And if we all shared them, *all* of us would be stronger.

It all comes down to trust.

Elements of Trust

So far, this has been a real bummer of a chapter. Nothing's sounded super great so far, and really, if you've been preparing to throw the book against the wall at this point, I wouldn't blame you. Don't worry, though, because here I come with the solutions.

Right now we find ourselves in the first step of the three-step process in the previous chart, which is efficiency. But we're efficient with potentially inaccurate data, so what good does that do us?

When we move to step two—collaboration—then we'll be working together. If we can clean and improve our data as a group, we can solve, or at least lessen, our accuracy issue.

Think about how many of your competitors have similar data to yours, but maybe theirs isn't corrupt. Consider who else in the industry has also experienced a particular phenomenon/delay/order.

We clean our data together, and we pool it together. With this, we improve it dramatically.

How about the tech? Well, the hardware side is always going to require backup, as that's just the nature of things. But one thing we can start considering is the reliability of the hardware that runs our AI stack. Computers and processors get better all the time. Between when I'm writing this book and when it hits your hands, there will have been numerous advances in the tech realm. And since the focus is on AI all the way around, that reliability is going to improve as well.

But trusting your tech also has to do with software, and for us, it's also AI. The cleaner and more abundant that our data is, the more accurate the AI will become. If we just stacked AI on top of what we already have with garbage data, we're going to get garbage output. But with a cleaner set, we'll get better results. To do that, we need to work together.

Which brings it all back around to relationships. Look, I get it. Making friends as an adult is hard, and sometimes you don't want to leave the meeting and go get drinks to try to network, because you just want to pass out on the bed in the hotel. There are plenty of times in my life where the comfort of a couch calls to me more than hanging out at some event.

This, however, is different. We should be looking at everyone else in the supply chain as our comrades. These are our compatriots in the field, and yes, sometimes they are our competition. I get that. But if we're able to share our information and learnings with those folks, we will all prosper.

Together, We're More Powerful

We can't have solid AI without collaboration, and we can't collaborate until we open ourselves up. I want to do it, but the other person thinks I'm bluffing. Another company decides to throw everything they've got into the mix to try to make collaboration happen, while a separate business calls their bluff. Sometimes the supply chain feels like a poker game.

The Way the Game of Global Supply Communications Is Played Today
We share as little as possible, hoping to gain an advantage

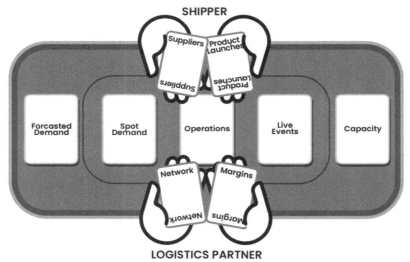

I think a lot of the resistance to collaboration comes from our natural competitive nature. We all have KPIs to meet (or beat) and people who want us to do better than the other guys. I hear that.

On the flip side, there has been lots of talk in the global supply chain world about having a control tower and more visibility. How do you think that is going to happen without collaboration? A control tower is there to regulate the global supply chain in such a way that things are done more efficiently. How will they do that without the right data? Easy: they won't.

What we need is more visibility. We need a common layer of data sharing in place that allows all of us to use it. How? Well, there are lots of choices, but maybe one of them is to anonymize the data. Keep it in an abstracted state, but let it flow to all the relevant supply partners. This stops all of the gaming and manipulation that takes place in today's system, because what we do today is an awful lot like gambling, and we need to eliminate that.

Think of the problem-solving that comes with this collaboration too. Two minds are better than one, right? If we see our suppliers, customers, and the factory as partners and co-innovators, think about the diverse set of views we can bring into problem-solving with us. By putting all of the players in one space, we become a team. And teams win.

We've had situations before when we've done just that. Years ago there was a scenario where customers found empty shelves in the beverage aisle. The retailers started sharing their inventory levels in stores with their suppliers, which allowed them to replenish faster.

Sharing is an opportunity, not a threat. This opens us up from our silos and allows us to look at the world as a whole, not just focus on our own "stuff." Collaboration lets us find patterns, which lead to improved AI pathways. Remember, better data means better AI.

And when that inevitable bullwhip occurs, whether it's from another pandemic or some other supply chain mishap, we will have the tools we need to move forward and solve the problems quickly, instead of pointing the finger and taking months or years to fix it. We need to think in the macro, not the micro. And that means looking to the future.

Looking beyond Today

We in the global supply chain tend to think of the customers we have. But what if we flipped our perspective a little bit? What about the customers that we failed to serve?

Once we start collaborating as a group, we will all gain more customers. We'll have better data to work with, and the customers that we gain, we'll keep. Why would they leave if we're serving their needs adequately?

It's not so much about collaborating directly with competition, as it is the fact that some of your customers and partners are also doing business with your competitors. This means it's about quantifying a gain you can achieve, getting comfortable with the certain degree of risk required to achieve it, monitoring that risk, and taking action if the gain fails or the risk occurs.

This also helps solve another problem. We're not tracking the quality and health of the global supply chain. Are things flowing properly? Is there a problem in a particular region? Is that hot toy going to sell out before the holiday season? If we share data, then we'll be able to know all of this information and plan accordingly all year round. We'll know if there's an issue, because we could establish things such as those health checks and show whether things are working or not.

Today, we look at things as a cost. Apple, for example, purchases their supply and determines their capacity years in advance. That boxes out the competition and helps them out long term. But if I, the supplier, can reduce my inventory and balance it such that I minimize the money I have into it, without losing sales opportunities, I can be ahead of my competition.

I can't be the only cheerleader for this kind of system, which is where you come into play. Some companies are sharing their data, but we need you to do the same. Tell others. Start a group that collaborates with each other and then expand to another. Get your people to understand that autonomous supply is where we need to get to and secure their buy-in.

That's the goal. It's anticipating the needs for a pencil, as I mentioned in chapter 3. Remember that? The concept that someday Amazon, or someone similar, will know that I need a pencil before I do, and so when that time comes, they have my favorite brand on the truck, ready to go. Autonomous AI. A supply chain that anticipates and works for us, making all of our lives easier.

Think about what we do when a bullwhip hits us today. First, we put a task force on it. Then we assign that task force to find a way to solve the problem so we can move forward. But that's all a very reactive way to do things.

What I'm proposing will make us proactive. We'll learn about the root cause of a bullwhip so we can potentially avoid those problems before they happen. We could reduce delays from weeks to minutes, but we all have to be on the same trusted level, treating our suppliers as true partners from the beginning and continuing through to the present day.

The Future Is Co-Innovation

I have this life plan. The idea is to live until I'm 141 years old, which ends up being the year 2112 (and the song referenced in the next chapter). Now I understand this concept is kinda nuts, and that's fine, but one reason I like the year 2112 is because on December 21, 2112, the digits go off infinitely.

The other bit here is that it means I look toward the future with hope, because it's a place where I want to be. It means I need to solve the problems of the future today, because the longer that solution is in place, the more rock solid it's likely to become. And that's powerful and motivating for me.

Co-innovation is key to that. I don't have the answers to all of life's problems, but I bet with the right group of people, I could be part of the solution. When we work together, we get co-innovation. We find better ideas and better solutions. We're able to balance supply and demand better, which leads to more sustainable businesses. And what does all that lead to?

Elevation. Naturally.

CHAPTER NINE

The Future Looks Good

We've taken care of everything
The words you hear, the songs you sing
The pictures that give pleasure to your eyes
It's one for all and all for one
We work together, common sons
Never need to wonder how or why.

—"2112," RUSH

Way back in 1957, Disney introduced the Monsanto House of the Future.[81] The idea was to show what life would be like in the maybe not-so-distant years to come. It had a microwave and all sorts of other goodies, but ultimately, no matter how well built the whole thing was, the home would close in 1967, just ten years later. It was a cool idea, but it needed further innovation.

---

81 "Monsanto House of the Future," Yesterland, n.d., https://yesterland.com/future-house.html.

In the early 2000s, I was lucky enough to become friends with another fellow future-thinking innovator, someone else who always lives in the future, a man named Jason Friedman. He's the creator of CXFormula,[82] which is a company that developed a concept called the Kinetic Customer Formula, or KCF. It's a way to grow and scale your business using customer success, and while I'm very much glossing over the idea, it's quite powerful in implementation.

Back then he brought me into his world, which was a new concept that wasn't really talked about and wasn't promoted: customer experience. The idea that you can design the experiences you want your customers to have no matter the industry.

Now he got his start straight out of college as a theater geek touring across the country doing various shows, and one thing he started to learn a lot about was lighting. He learned so much that the vendor of their lighting systems called him one day asking if they could fly him out at their expense. It turned out one of their customers had a big unveiling coming up, and nothing was working. Well, it turned out that big unveiling was the grand opening of Universal CityWalk in Los Angeles.

He got out there, and sure enough, nothing was working. He sorted things out, but in the process he saw this new kind of customer experience that was nothing like he had seen before. Sure, he had been to parks such as Disney World before, but they were just destinations. This thing, CityWalk, was a whole journey. It was a playground of shopping, eating, entertainment, and socializing being forged outside of the parks, bringing them together with the rest of the world.

This is when a light bulb went off. He realized he could help other companies deliver that same kind of experience. This turned

---

82   "About Us," CXFormula, accessed January 20, 2024, https://www.cxformula.com/about/.

into things such as the transformation of Foot Locker. New stores featured parquet basketball floors and helpful staff in referee uniforms. He also went to Bank of America and helped them with their digital transformation, using LCD panels to display information. This is the same kind of thing we take for granted at every airport and restaurant today, with menus and flight arrivals all being displayed on LED panels, which is the technology that evolved from LCD. Jason did this decades ago.

A little over twenty years ago, Jason came to me with a new challenge. Disney wanted to reinvent the House of the Future, but they wanted it different from one of their longer-running attractions, Walt Disney's Carousel of Progress. This would be a fresh, new experience at Disneyland. What could that look like?

Jason's idea was to make the experience a home tour. Disney staff would be tour guides through the rooms, and each space would change the experience dynamically once guests were in its presence. The lights would shift color, hue, or brightness level. The works of art could visually change what they were showing. The kitchen would display recommended recipes based on the ingredients being taken out of the cabinets and refrigerator. Everything would be dynamically engaging and unique to the people in that particular room at that particular time. It was absolutely transformative.

This was over twenty years ago. Today, you can buy a Samsung Family Hub smart fridge[83] that does the same thing. What was a far-flung futuristic idea is now available at Best Buy.

Recently I was at Disneyland with my family. We're usually an East Coast Disney World kind of family, but we were out West because my daughter was visiting Berkeley, as well as a few other

---

83 "Get Recipes and Plan Meals on Your Family Hub Smart Fridge," Samsung Electronics America, n.d., https://www.samsung.com/us/support/answer/ANS00087002/.

California universities. Conveniently enough, Disneyland happened to be centrally located for our excursions, so we set that up as our home base for the visits and sneak in some quality family time.

It also happened to be a great opportunity to finally show my kids this amazing innovation that Jason and I helped forge. But when we got there, it was nowhere to be found. I did some googling on the spot and realized that it had closed years prior.

Why? Because the technology was already out of date. The original House of the Future lasted ten years. This latest version was completely reinvented, futuristic, and dead inside of five to ten years.

Innovation is moving faster than it ever has before.

Exponential Growth

Do you remember VHS tapes? When I was a kid, they were everywhere. It was how you watched movies at home on your special VHS player. You could even record live TV shows on them or movies in your camera. They came out in 1976,[84] and they were a staple of my childhood.

But here's the thing: Betamax was better. Betamax, the competing standard developed by Sony in 1975,[85] had a higher horizontal resolution, the tape itself was smaller, and there was less video noise. But it lost the format wars[86] that ran through the early 1980s. There are lots of reasons why, but even though Betamax was often seen as superior, VHS was cheaper and could record longer. And that's why all of the Disney movies in my house in my childhood home were on VHS tape.

---

84   "VHS," Museum of Arts and Design, n.d., https://www.madmuseum.org/series/vhs.

85   Vanessa Boucher, "Fun Facts about Betamax," EverPresent, June 12, 2024, https://everpresent.com/fun-facts-about-betamax/.

86   Legacybox, "Betamax vs. VHS History: The Videotape Format War," n.d., https://legacybox.com/blogs/analog/vhs-beat-betamax.

If you then follow this down the home movie physical media track, with the exception of a brief blip with laser discs, we have the DVD.[87] This wasn't recordable—not initially—but gave users a smaller way to store their movie collections and in higher quality too.

That was 1995. In 2006, eleven years later, we saw the introduction of HD-DVD.[88] Just a few months later, in June, we got Blu-ray,[89] a competing standard that also could do high-definition video, and, like the Betamax, was developed by Sony. But this time Sony won the battle, and HD-DVD just lived on for two short years.

On Valentine's Day in 2016, Ultra HD Blu-ray hit the market,[90] with the ability to play 4K UHD videos. You can still find these discs in a PlayStation 5, and while there may be a world where 8K video becomes the next big thing, I'm not sure physical media will follow it forward.

Meanwhile, streaming video is developing in tandem. Apple's iTunes store gave the market streaming and downloadable HD video in 2009[91] and 4K HDR in 2017.[92] And of course, there were illegal ways to get these movies earlier, but let's just focus on the stuff that won't get you arrested.

---

87 "DVD," *Encyclopedia Britannica*, August 22, 2024, https://www.britannica.com/technology/DVD.

88 "Flashback: HD DVD vs. Blu-Ray," *Sound & Vision*, October 4, 2022, https://www.soundandvision.com/content/flashback-hd-dvd.

89 "Samsung Ships the First Blu-Ray Player," *PCMag*, n.d., https://www.pcmag.com/archive/samsung-ships-the-first-blu-ray-player-181068.

90 "Ultra HD Blu-Ray," Wikipedia, last edited September 22, 2024, https://en.wikipedia.org/wiki/Ultra_HD_Blu-ray.

91 Paul Bond, "iTunes to Offer Feature Films in HD," *Hollywood Reporter*, March 19, 2009, https://www.hollywoodreporter.com/business/business-news/itunes-offer-feature-films-hd-81012/.

92 "Apple TV 4K Brings Home the Magic of Cinema with 4K and HDR," Apple, September 12, 2017, https://www.apple.com/newsroom/2017/09/apple-tv-4k-brings-home-the-magic-of-cinema-with-4k-and-hdr/.

Look at how this all worked. It was almost twenty years between VHS and DVD. Then eleven for HD-DVD and Blu-ray, then ten for 4K UHD Blu-ray. The developmental cycle got faster every step of the way.

Let's take this same idea and apply it to music. You can trace the origin of vinyl records to the wax cylinder in ancient times, but really, it got its more modern start in the late nineteenth century, evolving from the phonograph cylinder. The disc soon became the dominant form.

Soon you could buy records in different diameters, which allowed you to sell single songs instead of a whole album. Different speeds were also introduced, but 78 RPM became the standard. And when electronic recording came out in the 1920s, it was off to the races. Soon they were all over, and it was how people listened to music—and still is, in some cases.

This led to more advancements. People like listening to the radio in the car, but a record player didn't really work. Instead we got eight-track cartridges,[93] which were a little before my time, but I saw them plenty in older cars. They came out in 1963, but the year prior saw the invention of the cassette tape.[94] Those would just dominate my childhood, and when the Sony Walkman came out? Forget about it. I could bop down the street listening to Rush all day long and love every minute.

But in 1982 the compact disc came out,[95] and once those caught on, I had a better way to listen to music. Then MP3s, then streaming—you get the idea.

---

93 "8 Track Tapes vs. Cassette: A Comprehensive Guide," EverPresent, April 4, 2023, https://everpresent.com/8-track-tapes-vs-cassette/.

94 EverPresent, "8 Track Tapes vs. Cassette: A Comprehensive Guide."

95 Erin Sullivan, "Compact Disc (CD)," TechTarget, last updated February 2023, https://www.techtarget.com/searchstorage/definition/compact-disc.

Again, it was decades between the record and the eight-track, then tapes caught on in the 1980s, CDs in the 1990s, digital in the late 1990s, and streaming today. Each time the developmental cycle got shorter and shorter.

The point is, there is always one technology that steps in to replace the former, and over the years the time between innovations has shortened a ton. I mean, think about the progression from the 5.25-inch floppy disk to the 3.5-inch floppy disk, to the Zip drive, to the thumb drive, to external hard drives, to the cloud. It took over a decade to get from the 5.25-inch floppy to the 3.5-inch. But external hard drives to the cloud? It was only a few years. The telephone went from Alexander Graham Bell to the iPhone in 131 years, but it took a century just to get to mobile cellular phones in the 1980s.

Everything moves faster, including innovation.

The Increasing Speed of Innovation Obsolescence

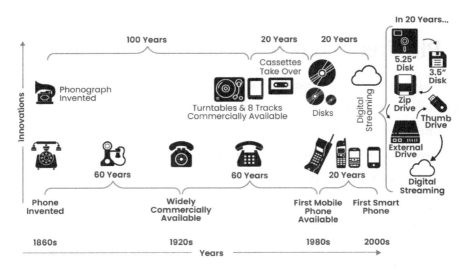

ChatGPT came out in November 2022.[96] As I write this, they're on GPT-4o, and everyone from Apple to Google has entered the AI market. Intuit, the software company that owns Quicken and Mailchimp, recently (as of this writing) let go of 1,800 employees.[97] Why? Because they're going to hire back *at least* that many to work on AI. They do tax and accounting software. Is AI really that important? According to this article,

> "The era of AI is one of the most significant technology shifts of our lifetime," [CEO Sasan] Goodarzi said in the opening of his email to staff. "Companies that aren't prepared to take advantage of this AI revolution will fall behind and, over time, will no longer exist."[98]

So who's going to be the Betamax of AI?

Playing Catch-Up

Walmart is a massive entity. It's been making hundreds of billions of dollars for a long time now. Safe to say you've probably walked into one before, and if you have, you know they're all about savings. They have such a large impact on suppliers that there's a term for it: the Walmart Effect. According to Investopedia,

96   Bernard Marr, "A Short History of ChatGPT: How We Got to Where We Are Today," *Forbes*, May 19, 2023, https://www.forbes.com/sites/bernardmarr/2023/05/19/a-short-history-of-chatgpt-how-we-got-to-where-we-are-today/.

97   Matt Ott, "Tax Preparation Company Intuit to Lay off 1,800 as Part of an AI-Focused Reorganization Plan," Associated Press, last updated July 10, 2024, https://apnews.com/article/intuit-layoffs-reorganization-ai-tax-prep-0fd5d4d4072fd2eb3a7bee04d820264d.

98   Ott, "Tax Preparation Company."

The Walmart Effect is a term used to refer to the economic impact felt by local businesses when a large company like Walmart (WMT) opens a location in the area. The Walmart Effect usually manifests itself by forcing smaller retail firms out of business and reducing wages for competitors' employees. Many local businesses oppose the introduction of Walmart stores into their territories for these reasons.[99]

Their buying power is legendary. Suppliers can also fall prey to the Walmart Effect, because they have to sell their goods for a price that Walmart is willing to pay, which means they have to push their own production costs down.

Walmart is a powerhouse, and in 2015 they brought in $485.7 billion in revenue.[100] That same year Amazon brought in $107.01 billion in revenue.[101] The math says Amazon made just 22 percent of what Walmart did. That's no small number, but it wasn't close to Walmart's gain, that's for sure.

Over the next eight years, Walmart's annual revenue would grow to $611.289 billion,[102] which it certainly does. And it was a pretty smooth rise, with only a small dip in 2016. Otherwise, they were

99 Will Kenton, "The Walmart Effect Explained, with Pros and Cons," Investopedia, April 28, 2022, https://www.investopedia.com/terms/w/walmart-effect.asp.

100 "Walmart Reports Q2 FY 16 EPS of $1.08, Updates Guidance," Walmart, August 18, 2015, https://corporate.walmart.com/news/2015/08/18/walmart-reports-q2-fy-16-eps-of-1-08-updates-guidance#:~:text=With%20fiscal%20year%202015%20revenue,approximately%202.2%20million%20associates%20worldwide.

101 "Amazon Revenue," Stock Analysis, n.d., https://stockanalysis.com/stocks/amzn/revenue/.

102 "Walmart Revenue 2010–2024 | WMT," MacroTrends, n.d., https://www.macrotrends.net/stocks/charts/WMT/walmart/revenue#:~:text=Walmart%20annual%20revenue%20for%202024,a%202.43%25%20increase%20from%202021.

doing great. How about Amazon? $574.79 billion, just under $36.5 billion less.[103] Huh.

If you look at their growth statistics, Amazon has soared year over year. In 2018 they had 30.93 percent of growth, and that wasn't even their highest number. In fact, they haven't seen less than 20 percent growth year over year since 2001 when they hit 13 percent.[104] The year 2022 was the first time they were under 10 percent, but they picked it back up the following year to 11.83 percent.[105]

Gennaro Cuofano, "Amazon vs. Walmart," FourWeekMBA, February 21, 2024, https://fourweekmba.com/amazon-vs-walmart/.

---

103   MacroTrends, "Walmart Revenue 2010–2024 | WMT."

104   MacroTrends, "Walmart Revenue 2010–2024 | WMT."

105   MacroTrends, "Walmart Revenue 2010–2024 | WMT."

Now I'm sure there are a million think pieces about this online, but let me put in my two cents. Walmart grew the way it usually does. It sells items for less and makes money on the profits. Amazon does the same thing, but it also has a very strong tech arm in AWS. As of 2024, it was 17 percent of its overall revenue.[106] Cloud brought in 62 percent of its operating income: $9.42 billion.[107]

But really? It's just more convenient. Yes, Walmart now has an online portal similar to Amazon, complete with a seller's market and all that. But Amazon is ingrained in all of our systems now. Want something quick? I know I don't want to schlep myself down to a Walmart and deal with actual people. I can just order it from my phone and have it sometimes by the end of the day.

The gap between the companies closed very fast. First, it was just a little, and then it went a whole ton quicker, paralleling the way technology evolves. In fact, Amazon may surpass Walmart by 2026.[108]

This indicates a change in how people buy things. Gone is the hesitancy of putting your credit card information online, and now people expect their goods on their doorsteps fast. It was yet another Silent Shift™.

What will be the next Silent Shift™? Is it companies such as Temu and Shein that forgo traditional shipping options and save by transporting them in bulk? Or is it someone else—a yet unknown player who has something lurking in the bushes that's not quite ready to launch?

106 Jordan Novet, "Amazon's Cloud Margin Widens on Accelerating Revenue Growth," CNBC, April 30, 2024, https://www.cnbc.com/2024/04/30/aws-q1-earnings-report-2024.html.

107 Novet, "Amazon's Cloud Margin Widens on Accelerating Revenue Growth."

108 Peter Cohan, "Amazon Could Soon Be No. 1 U.S. Retailer but Walmart Stock Has Upside," *Forbes*, May 16, 2024, https://www.forbes.com/sites/petercohan/2024/05/16/though-amazon-could-lead-by-2026-walmart-stock-has-upside/.

Fears and Fortunes

So far, all of these concepts seem a little bit scary. Our music media formats have shifted dramatically over one hundred years. Walmart is on the cusp of being upended by a relatively new company. AI didn't exist when COVID-19 hit, but now it is so important that corporations are firing employees just to get the head count room to add more engineers to build out their own LLMs. That amount of rapid change is scary.

It's also not new. The old adage about Henry Ford putting carriage drivers out of business has gone on for a long time now, and to a certain extent, it's true. When there is a shift—silent or otherwise—in the market, things will adjust accordingly, and people may lose their jobs. If you're potentially one of these people, you may have chucked this book into a fireplace by now, and you're using it as kindling. There could be a lot of people out of a job very quickly, and that's terrifying.

You're right. It is. And I know that because I almost played a part in doing just that to six people.

About ten to fifteen years ago, we were doing some work with the National Oceanic and Atmospheric Administration, specifically the National Marine Fisheries Service. We wanted to do something to help clean up our environment, solve world hunger, and all of those things using technology, which was, admittedly, a little bit ahead of the curve and ambitious. But the National Oceanic and Atmospheric Administration seemed like the perfect spot to make an impact, so off we went.

We started by focusing on one specific report, the Report of the Fisheries of the United States. It gets put together every year by a team of six people, and it's worded pretty much the same every year too. At its core, this is an Excel document with some macro-based tables.

The parameters are changed based on whether the number went up or down from year to year.

You don't have to be a futurist to see this is a great candidate for automation. Our thought process was if we could free up those six brains from doing this report, what other amazing things could they do instead? What else could they think about and create? How else would they contribute to making this world a better place?

Leadership shut us down. The problem wasn't that we freed up six brains. Instead, the management looked at it from a different perspective. If they couldn't do that spreadsheet, they're effectively out of jobs. Oh, and here's the part that really stung. They said they were not in the business of eliminating jobs from the government. They're here to create and sustain jobs.

On the one hand, I understand that nobody wants to get fired. But nobody was suggesting that. Our idea was to reassign them to something where they could create a higher impact, but leadership wanted them to stay status quo.

The other bit that stung about this was our idea wasn't just to change a spreadsheet's owners. We had a plan that was much crazier. We called it "Joe Globe."

Stop me if any of this sounds familiar.

We were going to take every form of data that we could—be it environmental, industrial, economic, or even the fisheries data—and we would combine it with climactic measures and overlay it with temperature and humidity or geological surveys, and we could do powerful things.

If we had a map of the seafloor and its structures, we could see what kind of impact commercial traffic had on the environment, whether it was boats or planes. We could map out a particular population of fish or other marine animal and game out what would happen if there was an adjustment in their environment or other contributing factors. Anything was possible.

We were definitely reaching way farther into the future than people were willing to entertain. AI was over a decade from coming to fruition, and still, even today, our ideas seem a little bit out there. But imagine the great things we could do for our environment with generative AI, the bigger questions we could answer with the power of a partner that's got all of those data sets in its collective knowledge. It could very well come in and give us answers that no teams of people ever could and then give us ways to take action.

Maybe someday "Joe Globe" will come back into action, but if it does, I'll hold the same stance that I did then: I don't think people should get fired. Instead, I'm proposing a different type of worker.

The Digital Worker

Today's LLMs and the future's AI ecosystems™ will still require human interaction. AI isn't good at everything right now, and it probably won't ever be. Humans are going to continue to do things that humans are good for. In some cases, that will mean hardware or software support for the AI ecosystem™. Maybe that's changing out hard drives or feeding in new data. But the new generation is going to be a copilot to AI (with apologies to Microsoft). We're not going to work separately. We're partners.

There are already new job titles coming out of the AI industry. Prompt engineers determine how to properly phrase a prompt for an AI system so that it responds to the question in a predictable fashion.[109] Today, it can be a little bit wonky to get the result you want out of a

---

109 "What Is Prompt Engineering?," Amazon Web Services, Inc., n.d., https://aws.amazon. com/what-is/prompt-engineering/.

chatbot. Asking it for the best chicken salad recipe is subjective, but if you ask it for the best chicken salad recipe that uses ingredients you already have at home, that might give you a better response.

Now you're not looking for recipes (although no judgment if you are). More complex tasks that involve the supply chain may require multilayered questions. They could need nuance, the kind that's only available if you ask the right question the right way.

You can train someone to be a prompt engineer. You don't have to fire your entire staff and hire new ones who are already prompt engineers or any of the other possible positions. If you have people on your team who are interested in taking it on, show them the path. It could be the best way to go.

There's also the possibility that you'll need other types of positions. One argument is that a prompt engineer isn't actually what you want. Instead, it's someone who specializes in problem formation.

According to the *Harvard Business Review,*

Problem formulation and prompt engineering differ in their focus, core tasks, and underlying abilities. Prompt engineering focuses on crafting the optimal textual input by selecting the appropriate words, phrases, sentence structures, and punctuation. In contrast, problem formulation emphasizes defining the problem by delineating its focus, scope, and boundaries. Prompt engineering requires a firm grasp of a specific AI tool and linguistic proficiency while problem formulation necessitates a comprehensive understanding of the problem domain and ability to distill real-world issues. The fact is, without a well-formulated problem, even the most sophisticated prompts will fall short. However, once a problem is clearly defined, the linguistics nuances of a prompt become tangential to the solution.[110]

110   Oguz A. Acar, "AI Prompt Engineering Isn't the Future," *Harvard Business Review,* June 6, 2023, https://hbr.org/2023/06/ai-prompt-engineering-isnt-the-future.

The entire article is brilliant and well worth the read. But regardless of your feelings about prompt engineering versus problem formulation, either way you need people to fill those roles. There doesn't have to be a carriage driver without a horse to steer. Just give them a car instead.

Putting People First

If you bought this book to find how you can be part of the solution to our supply chain woes, found out it was AI, and now are worried for your job, please take a deep breath. It's OK. We'll still need you.

There is very little doubt in my mind that at the beginning, when all of this is fresh and people believe that AI can do everything, there will be people fired. In fact, it's already happened.

I've got a buddy who was a copywriter. He worked for a marketing company on the East Coast, and while he liked the job, it had its ups and downs. Then in September, about three weeks before he was supposed to go to a conference for the company, he was told his job, as well as the other writer on the team's job, was going to be eliminated by the end of the year. The CEO had played golf with the owners of an AI start-up who convinced him their service could do my friend's job. The other copywriter quit on the spot. My friend was unemployed on New Year's Day.

He's doing OK. He's found another gig, so everything is fine for him. His new gig involves him writing about AI, which is a fun little twist on the scenario. Is he concerned about his career path? Sure, but he's also looking at ways of shifting direction in such a way that AI isn't his enemy but his partner. By doing that, he hopes to stay gainfully employed and doing what he loves.

I overheard this once in a meeting, and I'm not sure who exactly said it, so forgive me for the anonymous quote. But I was once told, "Nobody's getting replaced by AI—but you might get replaced by someone who knows AI better than you do."

This should be the outlook of anyone who worries their role will be affected by the implementation of AI. Humans are the glue that brings this all together. We're the continuity to be able to figure out the next latest and greatest technology to be deployed that becomes beneficial. Without us, AI is just a tool sitting on a virtual workbench collecting dust.

So yes, the future looks good. AI is going to help us solve some of our data problems and keep us moving forward. We're going to sort out the supply chain issues together, as humans.

This isn't going to be short, though. We may look at revamping the global supply chain as a long-term project with short-term goals. There's a lot of embedded thinking going on, and sometimes it's hard to break that habit. In the next chapter, I go into just how to do that and what the next one hundred years look like.

And who knows? Maybe by the year 2112, we'll look back at this time and wonder what we ever had to worry about.

CHAPTER TEN

The Next One Hundred Years

Time marches on …

—"FOR WHOM THE BELL TOLLS," METALLICA

I'm not a huge fan of car dealerships, but occasionally, I have to show up and get something done. In this case, I needed an oil change, and I just didn't want to be there.

The first issue is the new technology and marketing tactics that a lot of these dealers are using. They'll send you a text saying that it's Bobby or Sarah or whoever, reminding you about your upcoming service, but then when you reply, it's actually someone in accounting or an automated service that doesn't know anything about you.

This meant that I went into the dealership with a plan to drop off the car and Uber home. But I realized that I just didn't have the time to do all that back and forth, but I still had to take a call. I resolved myself to sitting in the sales room and hopping on a Zoom call because I had no other choice. I figured I'd be stuck nearby a bullpen, guys yelling out numbers like they're auctioneers, or hearing slimy salespeople talk about how they're really raking this customer over the coals. Ugh. It was going to be the worst.

I went to the service advisor, dropped off my Jeep, and walked into the sales area. What I expected to see was a bunch of different Jeep models, surrounded by cubicles and salesman. What I saw was a Lamborghini, a nice Range Rover, and a bunch of other cars that weren't even part of the brand. Were there cubicles? Nope. Barely desks, and even those were hidden away from view. I didn't even get tackled by a salesperson.

This is all about expectations. I went in there expecting one thing, and then I received something completely different. While I assumed I would be assaulted by salespeople about buying something new, I thought my space and time would be my own. Instead, I had a completely pleasant experience at the dealership, and the next time I need an oil change, I won't worry about it quite as much.

Now let's flip this to another perspective. I didn't see a whole ton of salespeople in the showroom. Is that because the dealer needed to hire some people or because we now live in a world with companies such as Tesla, Rivian, and Carvana, where all of the sales are done online? Where do car salespeople go when you don't need car salespeople?

This is the fear of change that is associated with AI. It's what we're going to see for the next year, decade, and century, and as the technology gets better and better, there will be people who lose their jobs, just like I talked about in the last chapter.

Like I said then, we need to figure out what the steps are to embracing that technology and exploring it, but we shouldn't do it on our own island. We need to collaborate with our customers and partners because these changes are coming. Let's work together to fix it.

Taking Care of Your Own House

At this point I've established that AI is the future, and we're all going to be living with it in our lives, right? But to make that happen, the other problem that I've brought up is how we get the data we need and then share it with other people.

Part of the problem lies with ERPs, or enterprise resource planning. As a quick refresher, when you run a large business, you have lots of pieces of software that do various tasks. An ERP gives you one consolidated system where all of the applications can talk to each other, which allows you to share data across different departments and people.

Now while I touched on this way back in chapter 3, the problem there was with the type of data people enter into ERPs. Sometimes the data is bad or mistyped. But in other scenarios, the problem is when ERPs can't talk to other ERPs.

My associate Gerald "Jerry" Ashley is the CIO of Ash Grove Cement Company, which was acquired by Cement Roadstone Holdings back in 2017.[111] One of the confines that he has to work between is figuring out how to get one company's data to work with another's.

Sometimes company mergers are difficult. Not everything flows together as nicely as everyone hopes, and there are conflicts.

Technology is hard, and even though one company has it figured out perfectly, that may not be the same solution for the company that is purchasing them. Look, sometimes it's just hard to make two disparate systems mesh up nicely.

---

111   "CRH Announces Completion of Ash Grove Acquisition," CRH, June 21, 2018, https://www.crh.com/media/press-releases/2018/crh-acquisition-ash-grove-completion.

Your Brain Isn't a Hard Drive

This is the result of disconnected conversations™. Think about how you get your information.

Right now, as I sit at my desk slapping away at the keys, I have my email and Slack open on another screen. My cell phone is to my left on my desk, face down but always available for a WhatsApp, text message, Instagram direct message, or any other kind of note I could get. Or, you know, it could be used as a phone, which is exceedingly rare these days. There's also a landline for the office and messages relayed through other internal protocols. Basically, if someone needs me, there are roughly two million ways to do it.

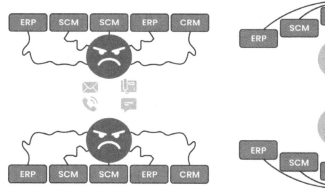

Once that point of contact is made, how is it recorded? If Jerry called me and we had a great talk about getting our companies to work together, where do I document what happened? Do I put it in a note on our CRM under his name? Does that flow into an ERP? Or does it just float off into the ether for me to remember somehow someday?

I know you probably think that you're superhuman and you can do it all. But your brain is not a hard drive, and it can't remember everything.

There's a great book that tackles this very idea by David Allen called *Getting Things Done: The Art of Stress-Free Productivity*. It gets updated all the time, and it's one of those classics in the business world. And a few years ago, maybe in a fit of grumpiness, he put out a blog post that more or less said, "Do it or get out."[112]

Actually, it said this:

> If you're not willing to commit to keeping your head completely empty, it's not worth trying to make any "personal management system" work. Give it up. Don't kid yourself. Throw your productivity tools away.[113]

The Getting Things Done system, as it's known, is all about Capturing, Clarifying, Organizing, Reflecting, and then Engaging with everything you need to do.[114] Look, it's a good book, and Allen doesn't need me to hawk his stuff. But there was a big takeaway that I had on the subject, and it was that your brain just can't handle all of the data you pull into it, and you can't expect it to be able to recall everything you need.

---

112   "Get a Grip on Your Process, or Give It Up," Getting Things Done®, November 21, 2017, https://gettingthingsdone.com/2017/11/get-a-grip-on-your-process-or-give-it-up/.

113   Getting Things Done®, "Get a Grip on Your Process, or Give It Up."

114   David Allen, *Getting Things Done: The Art of Stress-Free Productivity* (Piatkus Books, 2002).

In that blog post, he says this:

> But, hey, why not? Just keep it all in your head, throw away your calendar, and trust that you'll have what you need for information and perspective whenever you need it. If you had the guts to really do that, 100%, it might work. I might actually try that some day. Until then I will be responsible to the creative process that I'm born with, frequently making [sic] agreements with myself and others that I need to define, clarify, track, and renegotiate regularly, to get off my own back and to make meaningful things happen.[115]

I know I don't have the guts to do that. And while this is all about him and how he uses the Getting Things Done system, it is a valid argument. You can't just trust your brain to do everything you need when you need it.

The Integration Era Is Over

Which gets back to the original problem of communication, specifically disconnected conversations™. Jerry and I have a talk. Then we turn away from each other, and like responsible humans who understand that our brains are not hard drives, we enter all the right data into the right systems.

But what if we're not responsible human beings and we just blow that task off? Or, more likely, we're so busy that we don't have time to enter everything into a system. It just doesn't get done.

---

115   Allen, *Getting Things Done: The Art of Stress-Free Productivity.*

Apparently someone out there figured this out, and their solution was to create this technology called middleware with tools that allow us to create a plumbing of sorts between systems. This way a person could put something into system A, and then the "correct" parts of that data could be automatically moved, migrated, or ported to wherever they need to be in system B. This is what I call the Integration Era, and I would like to politely state that it's over. Absolutely done.

Disconnected conversations™ are no longer acceptable. Most of us have some kind of boss who tells us we have to do all that documentation, which most of the time adds up to completing a menial task that really isn't going to go anywhere. Your job shouldn't be parsing messages, thoughts, emails, and voicemails and then pushing them into very specific systems that very rarely get used. That's the old era, and it's the one I'm setting up to kill.

The new path is with Connected Conversations™. All the signals we need to sort out are within the conversations themselves. Rather than requiring an employee to connect to their own heads after each conversation, we can start sending the right signals directly into those systems automatically. People don't have to do it on their own. That means they can have more conversations and spend their time analyzing and interpreting the information they get, to create a much greater impact both in the short, near, and long term.

This is a complete transformation of the system, our jobs, and the way they're done. But this also means there may be some issues along the way.

Like the carriage drivers I talked about in the last chapter, we will need to evolve our workforce into groups of digital workers. These are individuals who will leverage AI as their own assistant or AI systems doing jobs independently. The combination of digital and AI workers will increase our overall team not only in size but also in productivity.

But that's just one part of the problem. The other issue that we need to address for the next one hundred years of work is the data.

Data Matters

Let's go back to Jerry and his problem with data. Some of the issues are with getting it into some kind of system, and others are about the data itself. That last part is key.

See, when people record data of any kind, they put it into a bucket. That bucket is usually determined by either the person recording the data or some specialist who decides what information goes where. The issue is sometimes there are subtle differences in data and where it's used, but unfortunately it usually gets applied universally.

"Everybody's got the same type of problems," Jerry explained. "What it all comes down to is everybody silos data. Everybody says you can't have this data because you don't know what it means. And if you report it this way, it's going to mess up the way I'm reporting."

Sometimes data means one thing; sometimes it means two. Sorting that all out is a huge part of the problem. "I spend a lot of my day going from sales to finance to operations to executive leadership, and the same piece or block of data means something different to each one of them," Jerry said.

This can mess with things such as setting sales goals. If you don't know how much something costs to move or the expense of a raw material, you can't accurately price things and then set a price.

One way of capturing Jerry's problem in microcosm is through the supply chain. At its core, the supply chain is the process of getting any item from one place to another. Jerry put it like this:

> How do you open that up in this data transfer to get people out of these secret spreadsheets to say, "I know to get something from point A to point B by this amount of time. I've got to make these hops [to get there]. Where is the real bottleneck?"

He works with lots of suppliers with lots of points along the supply chain. If one person is a bit slower than usual, he has to account for that on the other end, and he could find out who is the slower person using data.

Each of those points on the chain collects data from what they do, but what they say it does and what it actually means can be two different things. As Jerry put it, "We've got to strip to the raw data of what is *actually* happening and lay that out there and not have any preconceived notions on how you want to report it. You have to let the data lead the results and go from there."

Leadership and AI Ecosystems™

What needs to happen are two things, and let's address a large hurdle to start. Why isn't the data being cleaned up? Jerry put it pretty cleanly:

> Because nobody is sitting at the top and saying, "Let's just talk about some commonalities of what's important to us, and everybody needs to assume these things mean the same thing." And from there, you can do whatever you want, right?

Leadership needs to understand the problem as it stands and also needs to be part of the solution.

A quick sidebar here. Have you ever heard the old adage about selling drill bits? The idea is, people don't go to the hardware store to buy drill bits. They don't want the bits. They want the *hole.*

Drill bits are a tool to create the benefit they want—the hole. Which means if you want to convince someone to do something they may not want to do, explain to them the benefit. That's really what you're selling.

When dealing with a C-suite executive, you have to think about what the benefit is to them. What would they gain from what you're asking them to do?

I think the obvious benefit here is money. Keeping the shareholders happy is always important, and even if this is a private organization, nobody wants to throw money away.

Now we need to translate that by starting with the data. If someone in Jerry's position can get his data formatting to match with people at other companies within the larger organization, things become more efficient. And we all know how time equals money and all that.

But this also means more accurate reports. Executives would be able to predict things easier and more consistently, which makes their jobs easier. They get more information, it's cleaner, and it works company wide, even in each suborganization.

Now what's tricky about this is there will be a lot of meetings and wrangling to sort out these bits of data, and then the work of actually making things match up has to be done. Management may flinch at that cost, because it sure does sound expensive.

Creating AI ecosystems™ solves this problem, and it can do so on a large scale like Jerry is in. He's the CIO at one company that is a part of a larger company made up of smaller companies. Nobody can sift through all that information manually. An AI ecosystem can, though, which means it can sort the data into its own sets.

And then once all of the data is consistent across orgs, everything becomes much easier. Reports get more accurate. Data is cleaner. Money is being saved. Imagine what you could do if everyone in the supply chain did this.

Containerization

This all seems impossible, but if you remember, we've done this all before.

In 1956 Malcolm McLean designed the standard shipping container.[116] While there were instances where people used specialized containers before, even back to the 1760s,[117] this was a new universal method.

See, to McLean, the problem wasn't putting things into something larger and stronger. That was great. The issue was how they were built. Containers were made for trucks, trains, or boats but not for all three. It meant that you could get something off a boat and then transport it a different way, but you couldn't keep it in the same container from start to finish. Instead, he wanted something that could work on every vehicle. Don't design around *a* mode of transportation; design around *all* of them.

How successful was it? Well, back then, if you wanted to load up a container to ship, it would cost $5.86 a ton. (That's roughly $68 in

---

116 Anna Nagurney, "A Brief History of the Shipping Container," Maritime Executive, September 30, 2021, https://maritime-executive.com/editorials/a-brief-history-of-the-shipping-container.

117 "Containerization," Wikipedia, last edited October 1, 2024, https://en.wikipedia.org/wiki/Containerization.

today's money.)[118] But after McLean's invention? Sixteen cents.[119] Yeah. People tend to light up when you see that kind of savings.

Jerry wasn't there when that happened, but he did see how it became standard practice. "You look back and you think about how do we get to the point in supply chain of containerizing, right? How long did that take, and how did that get normalized, and how do you use those learnings to speed this up?" he said.

Well, if we were to apply the lessons of containerization to this new global supply chain problem with data and AI, we would look at what McLean and people like him did to get to that step. The cost benefits were certainly there, and it was definitely more efficient. But there was another bit.

Because they made sure everything was the same dimensions and shape, designing it such that it was stackable like a LEGO set, they made the container an unstoppable pro in a world full of cons. But to do all of that, they had to make sure if someone in China built a container, it would meet the same criteria as a container built in Boston. There's only one way to do that.

They established standards.

These Are the Rules

This is where the next one hundred years are really going to be cool.

As I've touted throughout this book, one issue we need to do is to get everybody sharing their data. But as I've laid out, sharing that isn't easy because everyone has different ways of creating and using data. Sometimes it's easy; temperature is temperature, right? But if

---

118   Nagurney, "A Brief History of the Shipping Container."

119   Nagurney, "A Brief History of the Shipping Container."

one company uses Celsius and another Fahrenheit, you're going to get different numbers.

This is where standards come in. There's an old joke about this one. Whenever two companies get together to figure out which of their standards is the best, they create a third one. This happens all the time.

But whether you're creating a third option or just using what's existing, this standard should propagate throughout the industry. We need to get everyone speaking the same language. Once we do, that's when the magic is going to happen.

Disconnected Conversations™ Drive Bullwhips
Every Delayed Supply / Demand Has Growing Adverse Effect Downstream

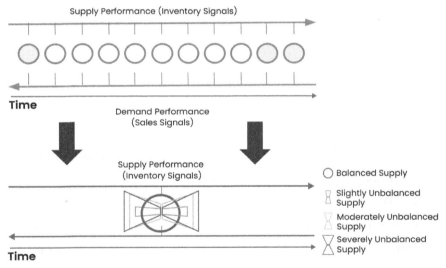

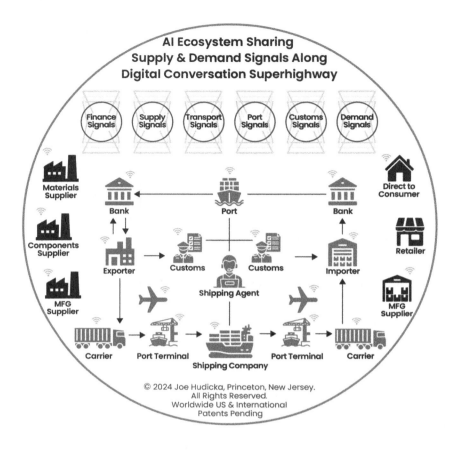

Put this idea together with the concept of digital conversations, and think about the expanded efficiencies across the entire span of the chain. Things start to move by themselves. Almost like you were moving into the third phase of automated AI. Time is saved, money is put into everyone's pockets, and we're all singing songs around a campfire while things are getting done in the background.

Sounds pretty great, right?

Look, I'm not saying that any of this is going to be easy. Fact of the matter is, it's going to be an uphill battle for a while. But the benefits are there. The reasons for creating this kind of environment are there. All we have to do is execute.

Is it going to take a bit of time to do? I think so, but it will probably ramp up pretty quickly. After all, time marches on, for whom the bell tolls. Now we just need to put this whole thing together so it makes sense.

Which is exactly what I'm going to do when we button this whole thing up in the conclusion.

CONCLUSION

Gotta make a change!
Gotta push, gotta push it on through!

—"REVOLUTION CALLING," QUEENSRŸCHE

Typically, no one gave the global supply chain a second thought until the COVID-19 pandemic hit. That person you see filling up at the gas station has no idea how the transition to containerization happened, nor does he care. All he knows is when he orders something from Target.com, it comes to his front door quickly.

But when everyone is running out of toilet paper, people start to question how things work and where the inefficiencies lie.

I think about this article all the time, titled "Shapes of Recovery: When Will the Global Economy Bounce Back?" It was published in September 2020 on Visual Capitalist.[120] You may or may not have a crystal clear image of what that time looked like, but that was when

---

120   Iman Ghosh, "Shapes of Recovery: When Will the Global Economy Bounce Back?," Visual Capitalist, September 16, 2020, https://www.visualcapitalist.com/shapes-of-recovery-when-will-the-global-economy-bounce-back/.

we were trying to figure out what the world looked like after the pandemic. The following winter we'd see some of the first variants, and it would all spin up again. We had no idea what the future would be, so we guessed, and that's what that article is about.

Of course, we did bounce back. Some countries did better than others, but we figured it out, and today things are mostly back to normal. But the problems exposed because of the inconsistencies in the global supply chain didn't go away. They were amplified during the pandemic, and still, nobody has fixed them.

We know these problems. The supply chain is designed such that if there's a problem at one end, it will be magnified by the time it gets to the other.

Supply Chain Communication Breakdowns
Disconnected Conversations™ Break Supply Chains

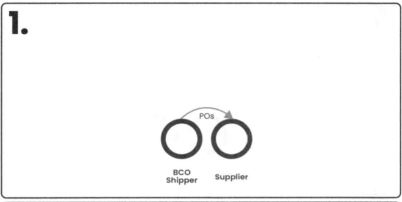

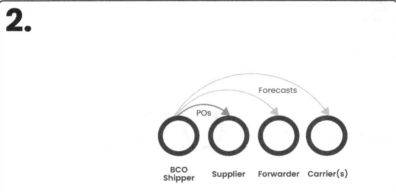

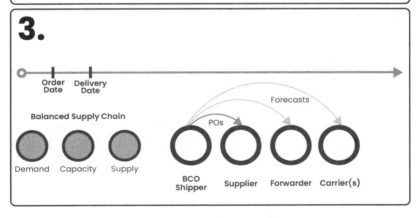

Supply Chain Communication Breakdowns
Disconnected Conversations™ Break Supply Chains

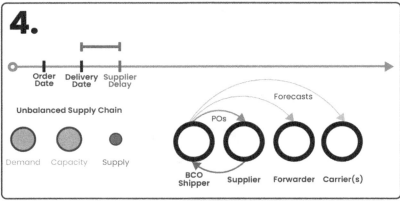

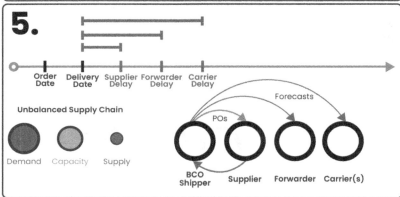

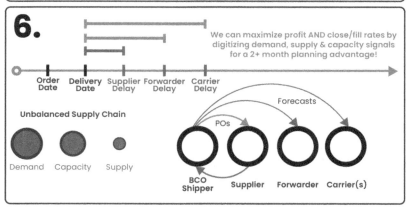

This can't continue to happen. We can't keep living in a global supply chain that has barely advanced in fifty years. We have to take big steps to move us forward; otherwise, come the next pandemic, everyone will be wondering how to buy toilet paper all over again.

You already know how to make it happen. But what you also need to do is look at yourself and think about the actions you can take to make things happen.

So let's do that. Let's make it happen.

My Friend

I know a guy.

Now I can't tell you his name, nor what he does, his age, location, or any identifying details. But believe me when I say this: I know a guy, and he's been both deeply inspirational to me and influential on my personal and professional growth throughout my life.

I understand that it's frustrating that I cannot divulge anything about this individual, but know that should you and I ever bump into each other on one of my international stops, and we find ourselves sitting at a hotel bar, and this topic comes up, I might be able to share a little bit more someday. Maybe.

So this guy that I know, his job was to maintain a certain type of equipment. He had to be sure these things ran 24-7/365, and he took the responsibility seriously. He wouldn't just read the manuals for the equipment; he would also memorize them. He would redraw the illustrations in the manual over and over until they were committed to memory.

Now this was before the internet, and back then we couldn't just pull up a website on our phone and see a diagram of the equipment in question. That meant my friend needed to know how to fix the equipment anywhere, anytime, using only what was in his head. At first I thought he was insane. But then after a minute or twelve, I really started appreciating it.

I would think about how great it would be if I were the kind of person who was that dedicated to guaranteeing success in what I do. Then the thought process evolved further, and I considered what it would be like if everyone on my team and my general ecosystem felt the same way; everyone was constantly driving for absolute excellence and doing everything we could within our own power to make that so. It was amazing and something I aspired to personally.

So one day over drinks, my friend told me about an exam he had to take for a training workshop on a new piece of equipment. It was a written exam, but he was prepared, so he wasn't worried. He took the test and felt pretty good about the results.

Before the instructor gave back the results, he stood before the class and said, "I have a problem."

He continued, "There's this one question that only one individual got right and everyone else got wrong. If I mark that individual's question as correct, there's only going to be one perfect grade for the class. That also means everyone else's grade will go down. Since this is an awkward situation that I don't want to feel responsible for, I want to bring this to a class vote."

Everyone in the classroom perked up their ears. They wanted to know what problem it was, and the instructor obliged them. The original question was an illustration followed by a question, so the instructor drew out the image. It was a light bulb with a wire attached, connected to a switch. The question read, "If the switch is flipped, will the light bulb illuminate?"

My friend was the only person in the room who understood not only that the light bulb wouldn't light from a technical perspective on this new piece of equipment but also why. He understood the mechanics behind the entire process, top to bottom.

The problem was, he responded to the question on the test with a simple, "No." There wasn't any explanation or reasoning, just the answer.

This was the instructor's issue. Had my friend put the full explanation into the exam, he would have gotten full credit, and there would be no question that he would get the right grade. But now this was a bit trickier. The instructor put it to a vote, and obviously everyone in the class was going to benefit if they voted "no," so that was what they did. My friend lost, but he was correct. It became something of a joke among his classmates and a core memory for all of them.

As my friend finished the story, he asked me, "How would you have responded?"

Now I've also found myself in some pretty crazy situations. Maybe that's because I'm the nutball who's coming up with radical ideas such as AI ecosystems™ when most enterprises are just fortifying their cybersecurity walls higher and thicker than before. But still, I wanted to respond.

Now I didn't know anything about the equipment, nor had I ever seen the manual, but I didn't think I needed to. Of course, the light bulb wasn't going to light. It was an illustration on a piece of paper. There's no electrical current or anything to light. Case solved. We both shared a laugh and had another round.

While this story means a whole ton to me, as does my relationship to this fine human being, there was something that I took away from it.

You have to be brave to be different. If you're going to make this kind of impact in your company, your ecosystem, and in the world, you have to step out and become an industry leader.

If you're gonna be brave, you've gotta be tough.

Disrupt

Napster changed the music industry.

It started as a peer-to-peer file-sharing service that exploded into the world. Soon "free music" was all anyone under thirty was thinking, and many a hard drive was filled up with MP3s of their favorite artists.

Sure, it was eventually sued into oblivion, but the horse was already out of the barn. People had thousands of songs at their disposal, and all they needed were inexpensive players to listen to them.

The digital revolution came calling, and Napster answered.

They weren't the first industry to make these kinds of sweeping changes in the digital era. Uber changed the way taxis work. Netflix did for movies what Napster did for music but with a business model. And shopping online at Amazon made that 1980s-era Sears catalog, which I used to pore over every Christmas, obsolete.

These kinds of digital disruptions happen when a market has grown stagnant. When the status quo is a pile of hot garbage and everybody knows it but *shrug emoji*, whatcha gonna do about it?

You change it. You step in and take a chance to make what's horrible better. You make a difference and shape the world.

This is the future of global supply. It's our digital disruption moment right here, but I can't do it alone.

I invite you to join us in this new world. Take our AI Ecosystems™ Readiness Assessment by scanning the QR code or visiting the link below.

www.joehudicka.com/assessment

Also, join us for a free discovery workshop where you can learn the intimate details behind their responses to the Assessment and how to turn them into strengths. You'll be able to implement your very own AI ecosystem roundtables with your key internal stakeholders, as well as your customers and partners.

So come with me, and let's make this a better world—together. Gotta push, gotta push it on through!

Revolution calling!

—"REVOLUTION CALLING," QUEENSRŸCHE

GOGOGO

Joe

CONNECT WITH ME!

Thank you for reading! I hope this book has inspired you and sparked new ideas. If you'd like to dive deeper into the topics we've explored or discuss how I can support you further, I invite you to reach out.

SERVICES OFFERED

Keynote Speaking: Engaging presentations tailored to your audience.
Workshops: Interactive sessions designed to assess and grow your AI Ecosystems.
Consulting: Personalized strategies to help you achieve your company's AI Ecosystems goals.

I love connecting with readers, organizations, and individuals passionate about growth and transformation. Whether you're interested in a speaking engagement, workshop, or consultation, let's collaborate to make a positive impact!

GET IN TOUCH

Email: Joe@joehudicka.com
Website: joehudicka.com

FOLLOW ME ON SOCIAL MEDIA

X: https://x.com/JoeHudicka

LinkedIn: https://www.linkedin.com/in/joehudicka/

I look forward to hearing from you and exploring how we can work together to bring your vision to life!